"The authors present us with a wide and varied bibliography that includes not only established authors, whom we may call classics, but also authors who are usually referred to as link psychoanalysts. This book leaves us with many questions concerning new families, what we mean by family, what clinical changes may unfold, and what are the features of the world that is opening before us, a world full of uncertainty. It is hence open to the future. While we can face this future with a wealth of knowledge already at our disposal, the authors encourage us to avoid being constrained by it."

—from the Prologue by **Janine Puget**

"In the light of the current transformations of hegemonic codes, how could the device created by psychoanalysis more than one hundred years ago remain the same? This excellent choral work, which brings clinical practice to the fore, offers a path that poses questions whose answers will be found in the encounter with the readers."

—from the Foreword by **Virginia Ungar, M.D.**, President, International Psychoanalytical Association

Psychoanalytic Work with Families and Couples

Psychoanalytic Work with Families and Couples rethinks the ways in which conflicts present today in psychoanalytic consulting rooms and the nature of suffering in family, couple, and sibling bonds.

Based on two major concepts, that of device (drawn from the philosophers Foucault, Deleuze, and Agamben) and that of link (developed by Berenstein and Puget), the authors have developed new approaches to clinical practice with families and couples that focus on the complexity, singularity, and immanence of patient-analyst interaction in the session. In thinking about link dynamics, moreover, they go beyond the consulting room to reflect on how these dynamics develop in other spaces, such as institutions, organizations, and the fraternal circle of colleagues.

Part I, Couples and Families Today, discusses changes undergone by families and couples in the last thirty years and their effects on psychoanalytic practice. Attributing a link logic to suffering and to the situations that condition it implies making significant decisions regarding our clinical strategy, our choice of a device and of an interpretive path. Faithful to the idea that the clinical dimension calls for transformations, the second part, Facing Clinical Challenges, includes clinical materials from manifold treatment devices that attest to changes both in contemporary paradigms and in the professional lives of psychoanalysts.

Psychoanalytic Work with Families and Couples will be of great interest to all practicing psychoanalysts and psychoanalytic psychotherapists.

Susana Kuras Mauer is a psychoanalyst and Professor at the Master's Program in Family and Couple Studies, University Institute of Mental Health, Buenos Aires Psychoanalytical Association, Argentina.

Sara Moscona is a psychoanalyst and Professor at the Master's Program in Family and Couple Studies, University Institute of Mental Health, Buenos Aires Psychoanalytical Association, Argentina.

Silvia Resnizky is a psychoanalyst and Professor at the Master's Program in Family and Couple Studies, University Institute of Mental Health, Buenos Aires Psychoanalytical Association, Argentina. She worked as Director of the Program between 2013 and 2017.

Psychoanalytic Ideas and Applications Series
IPA Publications Committee

Gabriela Legorreta (Montreal), Chair and General Editor; Dominique Scarfone (Montreal); Catalina Bronstein (London); Larry Brown (Boston); Michele Ain (Montevideo); Samuel Arbiser (Buenos Aires); Udo Hock (Berlin); Rhoda Bawdekar (London), Ex-officio as IPA Publishing Manager; Paul Crake (London), Ex-officio as IPA Executive Director

Recent titles in the Series include

Psychoanalytic Perspectives on Virtual Intimacy and Communication in Film
Edited by Andrea Sabbadini, Ilany Kogan and Paola Golinelli

Transformational Processes in Clinical Psychoanalysis
Dreaming, Emotions and the Present Moment
Lawrence J. Brown

The Psychoanalyst and the Child
From the consultation to psychoanalytic treatment
Michel Ody

Psychoanalytic Studies on Dysphoria
The False Accord in the Divine Symphony
Marion M. Oliner

Contemporary Perspectives on the Freudian Death Drive
In Theory, Clinical Practice and Culture
Edited by Victor Blüml, Liana Giorgi and Daru Huppert

Permanent Disquiet
Psychoanalysis and the Transitional Subject
Michel de M'Uzan

Psychoanalytic Work with Families and Couples
Clinical Perspectives on Suffering
Susana Kuras Mauer, Sara Moscona, and Silvia Resnizky

For a full list of titles in this series, please visit www.routledge.com

Psychoanalytic Work with Families and Couples

Clinical Perspectives on Suffering

Susana Kuras Mauer,
Sara Moscona, and
Silvia Resnizky

LONDON AND NEW YORK

First published 2020
by Routledge
2 Park Square, Milton Park, Abingdon, Oxon OX14 4RN

and by Routledge
52 Vanderbilt Avenue, New York, NY 10017

Routledge is an imprint of the Taylor & Francis Group, an informa business

© 2020 Susana Kuras Mauer, Sara Moscona, and Silvia Resnizky

The right of Susana Kuras Mauer, Sara Moscona, and Silvia Resnizky to be identified as authors of this work has been asserted by them in accordance with sections 77 and 78 of the Copyright, Designs and Patents Act 1988.

All rights reserved. No part of this book may be reprinted or reproduced or utilised in any form or by any electronic, mechanical, or other means, now known or hereafter invented, including photocopying and recording, or in any information storage or retrieval system, without permission in writing from the publishers.

A shorter version of this book was published for educational purposes for the IPA Congress, 2017 in Buenos Aires, Argentina. Thanks is given to Biebel Publishing House for authorisation to publish this expanded version.

English language translation © Judith Filc, 2020

Trademark notice: Product or corporate names may be trademarks or registered trademarks, and are used only for identification and explanation without intent to infringe.

British Library Cataloguing-in-Publication Data
A catalogue record for this book is available from the British Library

Library of Congress Cataloging-in-Publication Data
A catalog record for this book has been requested

ISBN: 978-0-367-31319-7 (hbk)
ISBN: 978-0-367-31320-3 (pbk)
ISBN: 978-0-429-31624-1 (ebk)

Typeset in Palatino
by Apex CoVantage, LLC

Printed in the United Kingdom
by Henry Ling Limited

To our colleagues from all latitudes
To Judith Filc

Contents

Acknowledgments	xi
Permissions acknowledgments	xii
Series editor's foreword	xiv
GABRIELA LEGORRETA	
Foreword	xvi
VIRGINIA UNGAR	
Prologue	xvii
JANINE PUGET	
Introduction	1

PART I
Couples and families today   5

1	Clinical devices	7
2	The suffering of couples and families	20
3	Family practice	26
4	Couples in conflict	31
5	Thinking about siblings	42
6	On clinical interventions	49
7	The fraternal dimension and trauma	62
8	Deficit and excess in contemporary life	77

x Contents

9 Exploring memory and forgetting   82

10 Sexualities in the plural: conflicting practices
   and representations   89

PART II
Facing clinical challenges   101

11 The psychoanalyst's writing process   103

12 Creating a link in the supervision space   108

13 Between analysts   118

   Bibliography   127
   Index   136

Acknowledgments

We are deeply grateful to:

Janine Puget, teacher and friend, for her generous prologue and her ability to promote independent thinking;

Judith Filc, our translator and editor, for her professionalism and her endless patience in this shared adventure of publishing in English;

Virginia Ungar, dear friend and colleague, for her availability to review our first book in English with great insight;

Santiago Kovadloff, for the intense and steady writing work we have carried out jointly since 1980;

the IPA Publications Committee, and Routledge for the careful reading of our book;

our students, who have been our faithful readers;

our friends, who always encourage us;

our patients, a constant source of inspiration;

and our beloved families, always there for us.

Permissions acknowledgments

A shorter version of this book has been published for educational purposes for the IPA Congress 2017 in Buenos Aires, Argentina. Thanks is given to Biebel Publishing House for authorization to publish this expanded version.

Chapter 1 – first published in Spanish (2002) in Chapter IV, Dispositivos clínicos [Clinical Devices]. In: *Psicoanalistas un autorretrato imposible* [*Psychoanalysts: An Impossible Self-Portrait*]. Buenos Aires: Lugar.

In Spanish (2014) in Chapter II, Dispositivos clínicos en Dispostivos clínicos en Psicoanánlisis. In: *Dispositivos Clínicos en psicoanálisis*. Buenos Aires: Letra Viva, pp. 35–52.

First published in English (2017) in Chapter I, Clinical Devices. In: *Family and Couple Suffering*. Buenos Aires: Biebel, pp. 21–38.

Chapter 2 – first published in English in Chapter II. In: *Family and Couple Suffering*. Buenos Aires: Biebel, pp. 39–46.

Chapter 3 – first published in English in Chapter III. In: *Family and Couple Suffering*. Buenos Aires: Biebel, pp. 47–52.

Chapter 4 – first published in English in Chapter IV. In: *Family and Couple Suffering*. Buenos Aires: Biebel, pp. 53–66.

Chapter 5 – first published in Spanish (2014) in Chapter XII. In: *Dispositivos Clínicos en psicoanálisis*. Buenos Aires: Letra Viva, pp. 35–52.

First published in English in *Family and Couple Suffering*. Buenos Aires: Biebel, pp. 67–82.

Chapter 7 – received the Elena Evelson Award for the paper "Lo fraterno en la tramitación de lo traumático" [The Fraternal Bond and the Processing of Trauma], co-authored with Susana Kuras Mauer, Sara Moscona, and Silvia Resnizky.

First published (2007) as Elena Evelson Award. *Psychoanalysis APdeBA* (Buenos Aires Psychoanalytical Association), 2 (XXIX): 395–422.

Chapter 8 – first published in English in Deficit and excess in contemporary life in *Family and Couple Suffering*. Buenos Aires: Biebel, pp. 103–109.

Chapter 9 – first published in Spanish (2014) in Chapter VI. Memoria y olvido In: *Dispositivos Clínicos en psicoanálisis*. Buenos Aires: Letra Viva, pp. 85–93.

First published in English in Exploring memory and forgetting. In *Family and Couple Suffering*. Buenos Aires: Biebel, pp. 111–119.

Chapter 10 – first published in Spanish (2014) in Chapter XI. Sexualidades en plural In *Dispositivos Clínicos en psicoanálisis*. Buenos Aires: Letra Viva, pp. 135–146.

First published in English in Sexualities in the plural. In *Family and Couple Suffering*. Buenos Aires: Biebel, pp. 121–132.

Chapter 11 – first published (2016) as The writing of the Psychoanalysts. *Journal of the Turkish Psychoanalytical Association Istambul*, 33: 127–140, co-authored with Susana Kuras Mauer, Sara Moscona, and Silvia Resnizky.

Chapter 12 – first published in Spanish (2015) as Espacio de supervision: trabajo vincular [Supervision: Creating a link in the supervisory space]. *Psycoanalysis APdeBA* (Psychoanalytical Buenos Aires Association), 37 (2–3): 247–259.

First published in English (2016) as Supervision: Creating a link in the supervisory space [Supervisión: creando vínculo en el espacio de supervisión]. *Journal of the Turkish Psychoanalytical Association Istambul*, 33: 127–140.

Chapter 13 – first published in Spanish (2014) in Chapter 15, Entre analistas. In: *Dispositivos clínicos en psicoanálisis*. Buenos Aires: Letra Viva, pp. 191–202.

First published in English in Chapter 13, Between analysts. In: *Family and Couple Suffering*. Buenos Aires: Biebel, pp. 157–168.

Series editor's foreword

Psychoanalytic work with families and couples: clinical perspectives on suffering

Susana Kuras Mauer, Sara Moscona, and Silvia Resnizky

The Publications Committee of the International Psychoanalytic Association continues, with the present volume, the series "Psychoanalytic Ideas and Applications."

The aim of this series is to focus on the scientific production of significant authors, whose works are outstanding contributions to the development of the psychoanalytic field and to set out relevant ideas and themes, generated during the history of psychoanalysis, that deserve to be known and discussed by present-day psychoanalysts.

The relationship between psychoanalytic ideas and their applications needs to be put forward from the perspective of theory, clinical practice, and research, in order to maintain their validity for contemporary psychoanalysis.

The Publication's Committee's objective is to share these ideas with the psychoanalytic community and with professionals in other related disciplines, so as to expand their knowledge and generate a productive interchange between the text and the reader.

The IPA Publications Committee is pleased to publish *Psychoanalytic Work with Families and Couples* edited by Susana Kuras Mauer, Sara Moscona, and Silvia Resnizky. The authors have done a remarkable job of tracing the changes undergone in families and couples over the last thirty years. They realized that there was a need to develop new family and couple therapeutic approaches that are capable of addressing new clinical challenges.

Consequently, the authors took up the challenge of developing a new therapeutic approach based on a theoretical framework grounded upon two key concepts. The first is the concept of "device" ("*dispositif*") developed originally by the philosopher Foucault and later by Agamben and Deleuze. The second concept is "the link" ("*vínculo*") developed amongst others by Isidoro Berenstein and Janine Puget in the River Plate (Río de la Plata) in Argentina.

The authors carefully explore these concepts in depth. They describe their history, as well as how they differ from similar concepts such as the psychoanalytic frame and the notion of link from a Bionian perspective. The authors also explain how the choice of these specific concepts enables a characterization of the diversity and complexity of present-day psychoanalytic interventions. The reader will find clinical material throughout which illustrates the different aspects of this new approach.

There is little doubt that the framework presented here provides important insights into the understanding of couples and family suffering. One should be thankful to Susana Kuras Mauer, Sara Moscona, and Silvia Resnizky for introducing a new creative approach to thinking about families, couples, and siblings and their suffering. I am confident that this volume will be useful and of much interest not only to the psychoanalytic reader worldwide, but to anyone interested in the complex and important subject of psychoanalytic work with families and couples.

Gabriela Legorreta
Series Editor
Chair, IPA Publications Committee

Foreword

A book in English about clinical devices that transcend individual psycho-analysis deserves to be celebrated, all the more so when it is a new work by three authors who have already presented the outcome of many years of thinking and writing together. They thus practice what they preach; by way of collective writing, they go from individual work to the production of a relationship that could be defined as a fraternal, professional, and, in a way, family link.

In a back-and-forth between clinical practice, theory, and technique, they firmly take hold of the notion of device. This notion has been under-stood, since Foucault, as a network of unstable relations among explicit or implicit heterogeneous elements (discourses, institutions, languages, ide-ologies, esthetics, and so on) that appears in emergency situations.

The use of this concept becomes meaningful if we think of psychoana-lytic clinical practice itself as a device. This practice comprises a series of heterogeneous elements and, like any device, emerges in relation to a new and urgent situation or, at least, a new situation. In the extensive and well-grounded clinical examples presented by the authors, the connection with suffering becomes natural. Suffering, moreover, can change just as subjectivity can.

In the light of the current transformations of hegemonic codes, how could the device created by psychoanalysis more than one hundred years ago remain the same? This excellent choral work, which brings clinical practice to the fore, offers a path that poses questions whose answers will be found in the encounter with the readers.

Virginia Ungar
President, International Psychoanalytical Association

Prologue

Throughout the book, the authors follow a basic principle – the need to acknowledge the creators of psychoanalysis without being constrained by their ideas. They consider it necessary to maintain their commitment to basic psychoanalytic concepts while incorporating new findings that appear over time as reality shakes the foundations of our discipline. Everyday reality challenges and energizes us, preventing the stagnation that results from exclusively advocating the explanatory validity of the past. The goal is to strike a delicate balance, and they have far exceeded this goal.

The authors thus present us with a wide and varied bibliography that includes not only established authors, whom we may call classics, but also authors who are usually referred to as link psychoanalysts. Among the latter, there are some who have chosen more traditional frames of reference, and others who have significantly distanced themselves from them. In addition, there are philosophers, writers, and social scientists.

A number of these philosophers have become part of the theoretical framework of many family and couple psychoanalysts, and are probably the ones who have most helped us open our minds and introduce new parameters to ponder human suffering or, rather, the shape human suffering takes today. As the authors state, we need to think that we are negotiating *a heterogeneous web*. This approach enables us to find new perspectives from where to question institutional life and the various modalities adopted by the politics of power and, doubtless, by our clinical practice as well.

The clinical examples that support their ideas are rich and interesting, and they allow us to follow the paths that led the authors to create manifold devices to address everyday clinical challenges. The way they present vignettes to round off each chapter is very attractive, and shows their strong commitment to their profession. They display great creativity in tackling difficult situations and find, in each case, the device that enables them to think along with their patients.

The clinical material they present is very diverse. We find parents without their children, couples that were formed in different ways, approaches xviii Prologue

to family therapy that include a therapeutic companion, the family treatment of a father with his two daughters, and other situations that readers will appreciate. Such diversity required that the authors revisit a concept that is becoming part of the psychoanalytic lexicon. I am referring to the notion of device, which is gradually replacing that of setting. The inclusion of this new term, which they amply justify, shows how everyday life forces us to question all those ideas and procedures that hinder our ability to do something with the present, that is, with the unexpected.

We can see, once again, the effort made by the authors to incorporate terms, concepts from other frames of reference that enrich ours. We could say that a different language is being spoken in this book, a new vocabulary has been incorporated that is necessary for those of us who work on what Berenstein and I have called "linking" ("*lo vincular*"), a notion that originated in the River Plate region and that many consider untranslatable. We should recall, however, that this notion brings together very diverse theoretical views, some that build on more traditional frames of reference, and others that fully break with them.

One of the chapters discusses the relationship that binds the authors, which dates back many years and has led them to write together extensively. In this process, they have experienced in the flesh the effects of a friendship that is conceived of in fraternal terms. It is a strong relationship that has resulted in a production based on love – a dynamic, productive relationship. They thus wonder not only about the complexity of writing in and of itself, but also about the difficulties and pleasures they have found in writing together.

The device they have created is unique; they meet for coffee every Saturday at 9 AM, not an easy practice to maintain. They slowly came to the conclusion that this fraternal group's writing constitutes an instrumental as well as foundational act. These terms are not exclusive because, above all, writing involves both faithfulness to one's origins and permanent transgression. Even if we show our faithfulness with quotes from the authors from whom we learned, we know that the act of quoting reveals a double movement. On the one hand, it shows our inability to incorporate the other's language in a creative way, and on the other, it is a gesture of honesty that protects us from the suspicion of plagiarism.

This is a great conundrum for all writers. Writing never starts from scratch, but one's writing shows one's own way of appropriating what belongs to others, which has actually been created to be appropriated. Writers need readers who can embrace their writing, but this is a complex matter. Appropriating is a way of paying tribute to someone who has offered something, but it can easily become an illegal or, what is more, a fearful appropriation. I believe that the authors must have undergone these experiences. Their quotes show their faithfulness to some authors whose theoretical frameworks make it possible to remain loyal to traditional psychoanalytic conceptions. Yet the weft they have created is certainly original and belongs to them, which means they have engaged in a creative appropriation.

The book includes long reflections on the notion of fraternal links, on which the authors have been working for a long time. They discuss the complex idea of a fraternal other who resembles us but is different, who allows us to recognize ourselves in him or her but breaks the illusion of sameness, from whom we want to differentiate in a gesture that cannot be completed. This type of relationship is what supports our friendly links, and it may also be forged in institutional life. The authors quote Dalí and Van Gogh, who had the misfortune of suffering the death of a brother, either before or after their birth (Dalí and Van Gogh, respectively). These experiences entail a singular relationship with life and death, but nobody could say that these artists were not creative.

Another topic that traverses the book is the role and vicissitudes of memory. The authors' reflection prompts them to coin a very apt term – conquering memory. It is a memory that may close the door to other cultures or take over the present, a memory that inhabits us and at times pervades us. This is an important topic for psychoanalysts, who are often so concerned with memory and memories that they cannot make room for a present with no history. Can analysts call memory into question? It is to be expected, but we are not always able to do it.

This book leaves us with many questions concerning new families, what we mean by family, what clinical changes may unfold, and what are the features of the world that is opening before us, a world full of uncertainty. It is hence open to the future. While we can face this future with a wealth of knowledge already at our disposal, the authors encourage us to avoid being constrained by it.

Janine Puget
May 2017

Introduction

Current chief complaints and new demands call for an expanded way of listening that has led us to develop and incorporate new tools and approaches, such as the notion of clinical device.

The concept of device derives from the term "dispositif" used originally in French by M. Foucault. Since this author did not object to its English translation as "device," we have adopted his criterion.

The diversity and heterogeneity of contemporary subjectivity has influenced both our conceptual framework and our clinical understanding and interventions. Furthermore, the emergence of new paradigms, and the social contexts in which they originated, have gradually brought about transformations in psychoanalytic practice.

The risk of one-sidedness and self-sufficiency posed by the classical models made us shift toward conceptualizations that rejected disjunction as the prevailing way of thinking. Contributions associated with the role of the event (Badiou, 2005) and the notions of presentation (Berenstein, 2001; Puget, 2015), deconstruction (Derrida, 1978), complexity (Morin, 1992), and connectivity (Moreno, 2014) opened the door to new approaches. In this context, based on philosophical developments around the concept of device (Foucault, 1994; Deleuze, 2006; Agamben, 2009), we ponder and revisit the referential polyphony that supports our current practice.

Theories on internal conflict, on the one side, and the intersubjective approach, on the other, refer to different modes of operation that are brought into play in different situations – legalities that interrelate and, at the same time, enjoy a certain autonomy. The study of linking realities requires us to be alert to the agreements and pacts that connect participants in the link and constitute the raw matter of unconscious alliances.

We are not referring to Bion's theory of linking. In the '70s, in Argentina, Pichon-Rivière, reviewed the classical theories (1971), and included the social factor in his operative referential conceptual schema (ECRO), emphasizing the relation between the singular, the group, and the social. He thereby gave the concept of the link theoretical status.

2 Introduction

The construction of the link theory to which we subscribe includes the category of the "other" as a fellow being, different and foreign to the subject.

The possibility to theorize about the presence of the "other" in the device and not only about its representation forms the base of a psychoanalytic link theory as we conceive it. We could borrow the words of Janine Puget who speaks in terms of a link (*vínculo*) notion, originated in the River Plate (*Río de la Plata*) region.

The relation with the other exceeds what is usually called the object relation. When we refer to object relations we are referring to identification and projection. The link with the "other," that is to say, the link between subjects, also requires a relation of presence, the latter point differing from E. Pichon-Rivière's contributions. Some issues are represented whereas others are presented in the link scene, producing effects.

In families as well as in couples, different evolving realities coexist and overlap. These are the realities of the couple link, of the link between each parent and each child, of the links between siblings, of the relationship with each family of origin, and of the interaction between each family member and his or her surrounding environment. In this way, heterologous, unprecedented logics emerge that call into question the causal, deterministic perspective with which we grew up and in which we trained, whose totalizing power is challenged by the logics of complexity and diversity.

The recent epistemological turn toward complexity engages us as twenty-first-century psychoanalysts. We are protagonists of this transition. We are being challenged to accept paradoxes, contain contradictions, assume risks, and maintain the tension between elements that we had viewed as antithetical. Change is no longer conceptualized as a transformation governed by causal, eternal laws, but as part of a process affected by chance and innovation. When Deleuze speaks of the device as a skein, a multilinear whole, or when we read that one of the consequences of a philosophy of devices is "a change in orientation, turning away from the Eternal to apprehend the new" (Deleuze, 2006, p. 344), we may conclude that complex thought brings the notion of device to life. We thoroughly discuss this concept throughout the book.

A century after *Totem and Taboo*, we have trained ourselves to construct sets of resources and tools appropriate for handling problems that today's society and clinical work demand of us. Following the tradition created by Freud, we believe that the culture of the present and the past unceasingly nourish the sensitivity and thought of those who practice this profession. Philosophy is a central protagonist in this influence. That is to say, this Freudian tradition presents a dual challenge: to maintain the conceptual framework of our psychoanalytic practice in its own specificity, and to constantly be open to the challenges offered by all that is new. Thinking about subjectivity in our times and approaching it clinically are activities

Introduction   3

stimulated by exchange with knowledge that may contribute to clarify the profile of our age.

The construction of a psychoanalytic link theory is not a natural fact, nor does it meet with consensus; it is in reality a novel fact that until relatively recently was inconceivable. Link clinical work is not content with proposing just one more application of psychoanalysis but seeks to account conceptually for the territorial expansion that has occurred in contemporary psychoanalysis. New epistemological contributions and interdisciplinary intercrossings feed and enrich our basic assumptions and strengthen the singularity of psychoanalysis.

We are ceasing to think in terms of essences, substances, or structures in order to account for the variability and fluidity of current experience. Today's psychoanalytic practice shows that we need to think in terms of transformations.

The treatments of couples and families, of links between siblings, and of other link combinations successively or simultaneously intertwine. Clinical devices are immanently developed and transformed, and hence resources multiply without forcing us to abandon psychoanalytic rigor. It thus becomes possible to vary the configuration of these devices within a single clinical strategy.

Modern thought fostered the hegemony of a universal law, a truth, and an essence that differed from the ones that had prevailed during the Middle Ages. Its theoretical models, traversed by the philosophy of splitting, were characterized by the reduction of the manifold to the unitary so as to undermine the autonomy of difference and prevent the new from irrupting as an event and causing unpredictable mutations. The logic of identity excludes difference as well as anything that is fuzzy, indeterminate, permeable, multiple, or changing.

The ability to abandon explanatory positions that postulate the hegemony of the Oedipus complex as the core of neurosis considerably modified our approach to clinical work. Had we not altered it, we would have run the risk of losing sight of current patients' profiles and of insisting on a biased, limited view. Analysts' frame of reference and the way we tackle challenges have also gradually changed.

We live in an age marked by the opacity and ambiguity of referents. Support networks are precarious and unstable, and we are intoxicated with hyperconnection. The figures that used to be invested with authority and ensured continuity have faded. Institutions are no longer reliable and have ceased to provide a steady sense of belonging. Undoubtedly, these phenomena affect the mode of construction of subjectivity and, hence, the way we inhabit our links.

Challenges to the paternal order, women's emancipation, children's rebellion, and the legitimation of same-sex couples have brought about changes in the organization of families. We are witnessing an increase in

4   Introduction

single-parent and blended families as well as in same-sex couples, and even the emergence of procreation without parents. There is an ever-increasing diversity in the modes of family configuration, and not every family involves a couple.

This book carries traces of the movement – sometimes seismic, sometimes not so much – that developed inside us as Latin American psychoanalysts. This movement generated the need to rethink the ways in which conflicts present today in our consulting rooms and the nature of suffering in family, couple, and sibling bonds. We have come a long way – from the couch to link scenes, from the neutral analyst who served as a recipient of patients' projections to the link analyst, who abstains but is not neutral and preserves his or her specific function in the immanence of the session.

Isn't suffering the chief complaint of subjects, couples, families, groups, and institutions? Attributing a link logic to suffering and to the situations that condition it implies making significant decisions regarding our clinical strategy, our choice of a device and of an interpretive path. Faithful to the idea that the clinical dimension calls for transformations, we have included clinical materials from manifold treatment devices that attest to changes both in contemporary paradigms and in our professional lives.

A second part of the book discusses the ways in which psychoanalysts tackle our discipline's ethical and clinical challenges. Our writing tends to give shape and voice to the itineraries of our thoughts. When we write, we aim both to harmonize the dialogical speech of clinical experience with our theoretical references, and to share experiences. Writing is showing.

Supervision provides another linking space of support, where analysts' obstacles, resistances, and ideologies can be reviewed. It is a place where theories are checked against clinical experience and then reformulated, a place that is suitable for the transmission of psychoanalysis. We also offer some thoughts concerning the way psychoanalysts interrelate. Institutional life, the value of belonging, and the peer connections that are developed in our institutions can help us reflect on our profession.

Now that psychoanalysis has entered its second century of life, we need to create new spaces and ways of working with each other. Sharing our experiences with our colleagues contributes, among other things, to preserving our openness to the unconscious.

Part I

Couples and families today

Chapter 1

Clinical devices

Philosophies of devices

To ponder twenty-first century psychoanalysis, we must consider both its foundations and the changes it has undergone over time. Current subjectivity conflicts and the way they are expressed through symptoms, our culture's anxieties and discontents, and subjects' need for the support of fraternal wefts are part of this book's itinerary. Conceiving of psychoanalysis as a *heterogeneous network* entails prioritizing not only the theoretical-clinical aspect of our practice, but also institutional life, the politics of power, and the *focal points of resistance*, which are also its raw material.

According to Foucault, subjectivity, knowledge, and power are interconnected chains of variables whose boundaries are poorly defined. This author seeks to analyze the mechanisms whereby power is wielded. In contrast to the caricature of an essentially repressive power, Foucauldian analysis brings to light the latter's eminently productive nature, insofar as it constitutes a play of forces that transcend violence. It is no longer a power that "makes die and lets live" but, instead, a power to "make live and to let die" (Foucault, 2003, p. 240), in other words, a "biopower." Its productive dimension is inextricably bound to another of its constituting traits – its capillarity. In fact, Foucault does not see power as the practice of a mode of domination emanating from a single transcendent, centralized point. Rather, power traverses the entire social fabric through myriad small centers and is exerted across them. This is what the French philosopher calls the *microphysics* of power.

Our clinical practice challenges us to understand how this microphysical biopower operates in the various devices we inhabit and guides our interventions. When we listen to our patients today we are listening not only to the vicissitudes of transference, but also to the link mode of patients with significant figures in their environment, the contingencies of our historical period, and the context in which we are all immersed.

We need to consider twenty-first century psychoanalysis in view of its original fundamentals and also the transformations produced in it as a

8 Couples and families today

result of its immersion in the cultural context of its epoch and the general training of its professionals.

The notion of device was introduced by Foucault and taken up again by authors such as Deleuze and Agamben. We believe that their reflections around this notion constitute a good starting point for our inquiry because they resonate with our ways of practicing psychoanalysis.

The concept of device[1] in Foucauldian thought refers to "the set of practices and mechanisms . . . that aim to face an urgent need and to obtain an effect" (Agamben, 2009, p. 8). Foucault defined it as follows in "Knowledge and Truth":

> What I'm trying to single out with this term is, first and foremost, a thoroughly heterogeneous set consisting of discourses, institutions . . . laws . . . scientific statements, philosophical, moral, and philanthropic propositions – in short, the said as much as the unsaid. Such are the elements of the apparatus. The apparatus itself is the network that can be established between these elements.
>
> (quoted in Agamben, ibid., p. 2)

Based on this definition, we would like to highlight three features of the device, namely, its strategic nature, heterogeneity, and reticular quality. *We argue that in each clinical case, opting for a specific approach involves the construction of a device that weaves together a network of variables spanning a wide range, from the vicissitudes of the transference to socio-cultural marks.*

Device, in this sense, means the materialization in a specific system of this network of unpredictable connections among singular elements. For instance, a man with a fishing rod constitutes a device, and the same man with a fork, a different device. In other words, elements change depending on the relationships – the connections – they establish with other elements. The device, then, is a system, a network of relations whereby singular elements acquire and produce new significations. With regard to our clinical work, individual, couple, family, and sibling interviews may be part of the same device. Each of these alternatives will shed light on different areas in the web of links.

Deleuze analyzes each of the lines making up the device and draws some conclusions. He argues that devices are

> composed of lines of visibility, utterance, lines of force, lines of subjectivation, lines of cracking, breaking and ruptures that all intertwine and mix together and where some augment the others or elicit others through variations and even mutations of the assemblage. Two important consequences ensue for a philosophy of apparatuses. The

first is a repudiation of universals. . . . The second . . . is a change in orientation, turning away from the Eternal to apprehend the new.

(Deleuze, 2006, pp. 343–344)

As psychoanalysts, we reject universals in two different ways. We are concerned with the uniqueness of each case, and we advocate for the need to make room for the new, that is, for what lies outside repetition.

The device: a skein

"First of all," stresses Deleuze when he defines the device,

> it is a skein, a multilinear whole. It is composed of lines of different natures. The lines in the apparatus do not encircle or surround systems that are each homogenous in themselves, the object, the subject, language, etc., but follow directions, trace processes that are always out of balance.

(Deleuze, 2007, p. 338)

A skein is something that presages more than one potential fate. In any case, it lends itself to be turned into something. For instance, it is, potentially, a sweater. It can transform into something new. Yet the weave is not there at first; it must be woven. Such degree of novelty and unpredictability justifies the need to organize the devices with the right balance between rigor and plasticity to allow for transformation.

The lines of a device "trace processes that are always out of balance. . . . Each line is broken, subject to *changes in direction*, bifurcating and forked, and subjected to *derivations*" (Deleuze, ibid., p. 338; author's emphasis). Balance is always unstable. This description by Deleuze offers a very clear visual and conceptual representation of the intricacy and complexity of the itineraries of a device. Once constituted, notes Castro (2004), the device will be subject to a functional overdetermination process whereby positive or negative, wanted or unwanted effects will resonate or conflict with each other and demand a readjustment. Deleuze, in turn, states that "the first two dimensions of an apparatus or the ones that Foucault first extracted are the curves of visibility and the curves of utterance." According to Foucault's analysis, devices are like Roussel's machines; "they are machines that make one see and talk" (Deleuze, 2007, p. 50).

Now, based on the notion of device, what does it mean to make someone see and talk in psychoanalysis? How do we situate ourselves as analysts? We are interested in Deleuze's proposal because it allows us to view subjectivity as the effect of a weft that facilitates different modes of addressing conflict, symptoms, trauma, and mourning. It is worth recalling here

10 Couples and families today

the conclusion of one of Freud's last lectures: "We cannot do justice to the characteristics of the mind by linear outlines like those in a drawing or in primitive painting, but rather by areas of color melting into one another as they are presented by modern artists" (Freud, 1933, p. 79).

Hospitality of the psychoanalytic device

Inspired by Derrida, A. M. Fernández describes two aspects of "the hospitality of the psychoanalytic device." One has to do with the need to maintain unique modes of approach. The other, to the need to inquire into the analyst's engagement in each case, that is, "the ongoing questioning of naturalizations or concealments of the patient's way to approach life, gender positioning, sex choice, age group, and so on" (Fernández et al. 2014, p. 23), which are closely tied to socio-historic conditions. In keeping with these formulations, we view clinical devices as complex montages, joint constructions produced by analyst and patient where the link is what brings to light the various configurations of the device. In other words, *the device is a product of the analytic link in the transference that, unlike the setting, does not precede it* (Mauer, Moscona, and Resnizky, 2002).

It is our contention that each device is built jointly and collaboratively. It is not preconfigured, nor is it fixed; it can vary depending on immanent rules. The key to its validation lies in the a posteriori reading of its effects. The device, then, is a creation "by two or more than two" that facilitates the emergence of unprecedented possibilities. The lines of subjectivation, to return to Foucault's term, would be those that ensure movement and openness; they oppose the idea of immobility. A line of subjectivation "is a process of individuation that . . . eludes both established lines of force and constituted knowledge. It is a kind of surplus value" (Deleuze, 2007, p. 341). This diverse configuration of subjectivity is akin to Foucault's view of subjectivity as perpetually being constituted, a process whose outcome is the opening of a space where to reflect on an art of living (Castro, 2004).

Cartographies of the psychoanalytic field

Clinical devices, then, may be viewed as instruments at the analyst's disposal within a framework configured by pacts and agreements whose terms have been jointly defined by patient and analyst. These devices foster the conditions for symbol formation and subjectivation that promote the unfolding of the analytic situation.

Complexity is characterized by ongoing transformation. Its greatest feature is its openness to the creation of a "custom-made" strategy. Thanks to self-organizing processes, each device sets its own course, defines its goals, and transcends the reductions caused by fragmentation. The purpose is to listen to human suffering. According to Freud,

> We are threatened with suffering from three directions: from our own body, which . . . cannot do without pain and anxiety as warning signals; from the external world, which may rage against us with overwhelming and merciless forces of destruction; and finally from our relations to other men. The suffering which comes from this last source is perhaps more painful to us than any other.
>
> (Freud, 1930, p. 77)

Expanded devices, which result from multidisciplinary and interdisciplinary approaches, have not erased the specificities of psychoanalytic practice. Rather, they have greatly expanded its scope.

As Foucault has said so well, claims Deleuze, "untangling the lines of an apparatus means, in each case, preparing a map, a cartography, a survey of unexplored lands" (Deleuze, 2007, pp. 338–339). This is what he calls "field work." Nothing could be more akin to psychoanalytic practice than the need to develop with each patient a custom-made device – *tailler sur mesure*. Alert to the suffering of those seeking analysis, we are ready to develop a cartography, to trace the outline of the device along with them.

"One has to be positioned on the lines themselves," adds Deleuze, "and these lines do not merely compose an apparatus but pass through it" (Deleuze, 2007, p. 339). "We belong to these apparatuses and act in them," he states later on. The currency of an apparatus is its newness, and history "is the archive, the design of what we are and cease being while the current is the sketch of what we will become" (Deleuze, ibid., p. 345). It is not about "predicting, but [about] being attentive to the unknown knocking at the door" (Deleuze, ibid., p. 346).

It should be noted that what appeals to us about the notion of device is the diversity of its components and the relationships among them. Psychoanalytic institutions and our ways of belonging to them – commitment to transmission, our continuing professional development, writing, conferences – all are part of the psychoanalytic device and form the network that constitutes it. We are not extrapolating from philosophy but finding a different way of looking at our field. The texture, elasticity, and consistency of a device feed on the creativity of a group. A variety of combinations can be generated that, paraphrasing Foucault, present not only lines of subjectivation but also lines of fissure and fracture. The rules governing devices are situational. The rule consists in creating the rule.

Stretches and/or modules of the web

If devices vary, if their effects are examined after the fact, we are faced with a temporality that differs from that of the process – with a temporality of stretches. It becomes necessary, therefore, to distinguish between two notions. From the perspective of process, the stretch is a segment that

12 Couples and families today

is part of a straight line, a line that is configured as part of a totality. A process comprises logical moments. There exists, therefore, a continuous sequence because by definition, process means that everything changes except for the condition that enables everything to change. In a process, successive moments are gradually woven into a sequence that has a beginning and an end. The Hegelian concepts of fundamental continuity, linear time, and single meaning allude to this notion.

Yet progression can also be thought in terms of modules, of units that make up a weft. Thinking in terms of modules entails an epistemological break with the idea of continuity. Each module has intrinsic production value; each contributes to the construction of the device. It is thus evident that the ideas of a module-weft and of the construction of the device interact harmoniously. The multiplication of devices is simultaneous with the increased complexity of reading tools and of the skills needed to interpret each module. Switching devices makes it possible to access opaque or mute zones that could not be perceived otherwise. At this stage it becomes necessary to distinguish between setting and device.

Setting and device: differences

The notion of device differs, therefore, from Bleger's classic definition of setting as a set of "constants within the framework of which the process takes place" (Bleger, 2013, p. 228).[2] In his book *Fundamentals of Psychoanalytic Technique*, Etchegoyen defines it as "an objective fact that the analyst proposes (in the contract) and that the analysand will progressively cover with his fantasies" (Etchegoyen, 1999, p. 532). The idea of the device as a joint strategic construction between analyst and patient is significantly different from these definitions. It is interesting to point out that Freud referred both to the constants of the frame and to the analyst's "mental attitude" (Freud, 1912a, p. 114), a concept that was later taken up again by Meltzer (1967) to discuss its implications.

Bleger argues that what is deposited in the immobility of the setting is primarily psychotic anxieties. Consequently, analysts should consider and pay attention to the muteness of the setting. Nonetheless, while he acknowledges that variation may give rise to new configurations, he warns analysts about changing the setting. He rejects the idea that we may judge these modifications by their effects. Etchegoyen, in turn, claims that unlike ever-changing variables, the setting "changes slowly, with autonomy and never as a function of the variables of the process" (Etchegoyen, 1999, p. 527).

Laplanche (1996) shares this view. According to this author, every action performed upon the setting should be considered an acting-out on the part of the analyst. However, he acknowledges that it is legitimate to modify the setting in order to adjust to changes in the real world, for instance, inflation, which makes it necessary to raise one's fees. From this viewpoint, the setting is still the stable container that is indispensable for the analytic process to unfold. Although closely related, setting and process are clearly differentiated.

The idea of viewing the analytic situation as a "dynamic field" (Baranger and Baranger, 1961–1962) traversed by lines of force originating in both analyst and analysand has certainly enriched the notion of setting. Even so, we should not equate setting and device. As we understand it, the setting is part of the device. It is not our intention to engage in a thorough discussion of the notion of setting or of the vicissitudes of this notion since Freud. We have chosen, instead, the concept of clinical device because it allows us to describe the diversity and complexity of present-day psychoanalytic interventions. We should also add the proviso that there is a significant difference between the psychoanalytic device, which is conceived of and developed for a specific clinical situation, and the Foucauldian device, which is structurally constituted and is intended to regulate the social body.

We have included in this book a number of vignettes where an array of clinical devices were employed, among them, joint interviews with identical twin girls, the temporary inclusion of a brother to enable diagnosis when a patient refused to attend without him, treating the parents in the absence of the son with whom the conflict had developed, couple therapy, family treatment with the inclusion of a therapeutic companion, and family treatment of a father with his two daughters. These clinical narratives show that *device* does not refer only to manifold treatment variants and combinations, but also to other dimensions of clinical practice that transcend the setting. *We are interested in using clinical examples to illustrate some of the ideas that underlie this conceptual experience. The cases presented below reflect the immanent construction of various clinical devices via the transference.*

First clinical narrative: a family – leaving immobility behind

This section starts with the medical history of a family treatment. The family was treated with a device that comprised both link work with the parents, the family, and the neurologist, and the incorporation of a therapeutic companion. Each of the strategies making up this device illuminated areas that would have otherwise remained invisible. In this way, new readings and modes of intervention became possible.

The parents of Elena, who is two and a half, have been referred to the analyst by a neurologist because the girl does not walk or crawl. Neither does she make any efforts to stand up. Attempts to make her do so fail because she cannot hold herself up. Her knees "buckle," as if she had no muscle tone. Elena barely moves from a sitting position. She only turns around when something attracts her attention or she needs to reach a toy. Moreover, if she has to lie down to reach the toy, she does not sit up on her own. Neither does she use her arm muscles.

14 Couples and families today

Comprehensive tests have shown no organic or neurological damage that would justify Elena's behavior. Her parents are puzzled. The fact that neurological causes were ruled out has increased their anxiety. Carlos, the father, is 44, and Estela, the mother, 42. Elena is their first child. The mother confesses that raising her daughter is not easy. "I was old when I had her; I thought I wouldn't be able to have children. I get very nervous when she cries or throws a tantrum. I quit work when she was born."

They live with the maternal grandmother, who is ill. "She has incontinence and arteriosclerosis. She's always lying down or sitting." Carlos adds that they had to move to the grandmother's home because he was swindled and lost the apartment where they used to live. It is not clear if Estela quit work to care for Elena or for her mother. The parents say their daughter barely speaks but understands everything. She likes books: "She looks at them, turns the pages. She pretends she's reading. She's like that because she's always with grown-ups." They are not worried by the girl's lack of speech.

Elena comes to the first interview in her father's arms. She is dressed in somewhat "old-fashioned" clothes that are slightly big for her. They sit her on the floor with her back to the analyst. She rapidly turns around, looks at the analyst with an intelligent, penetrating gaze, and starts hitting the floor with her legs. She shows the analyst that she knows what her problem is, what prompted her parents to seek help. Then she starts taking the toys out of the basket just to look at them. She puts them near her. If one rolls too far, she signals her parents to get it for her. She does not play, and is surrounded by objects that make it increasingly harder for her to move.

The analyst and the family jointly design a clinical device that includes a series of family interviews and the incorporation of a therapeutic companion for the girl. The therapeutic companion's valuable assessment of the family dynamics constitutes a key tool during the evolution of the treatment because it provides contextual descriptions. She finds out that Elena sleeps in the living room of the two-bedroom apartment. The parents sleep in one bedroom, and the grandmother in the other one. Elena spends most of the time in her crib, which is cluttered with toys.

The apartment is dark; the blinds are usually down, and there are many big pieces of furniture. The mother prefers Elena to be in the crib instead of the floor. There is almost no room for the girl to move around. The therapeutic companion quickly perceives "Grandmother's smell," an acrid mix of urine and lack of hygiene that permeates the whole place. She also witnesses the ritual surrounding Elena's potty training. To "help" her daughter, the mother lies her down on the dining room table with her diaper on.

In cases of severe developmental disorders, it is common to find an indiscriminate use of spaces that have been naturalized as part of the family's everyday functioning. The family fails to discriminate between inside and outside and between allowed and banned, among other categories. Furthermore, the process whereby children acquire new habits shows flaws and distortions that prevent normal developmental acquisitions. In this particular case, the incorporation of a therapeutic companion broadens the scope of observation and transmission, thus increasing the consistency of the assessment. She often sees relevant aspects of family functioning that are not brought to the session because they have been naturalized.

Elena's delayed walking and speech and her arrested development denote the presence of conflict. On one side, she shows difficulties to separate and become independent. On the other, the parents have a hard time providing adequate conditions for development. The surrounding environment could not adjust to Elena's movement and developmental needs. Her mother's fears, her father's depression, and her grandmother's incapacitating illness did not facilitate expansion, autonomy, or the right to talk.

The parents' anxiety regarding the possibility that their daughter may move around gradually emerges in the link interviews. Fantasies appear associated with the loss of control – the fear that outside the boundaries of the crib, Elena could start running "madly" through the apartment and bump against the furniture. The parents repeatedly allude to the dread of dealing with Elena's adolescence, which will find them "very old." They connect growing up with dangers they feel unable to face.

Some of the fantasies at play, which led to their unwittingly preventing their daughter's movement, are also revealed in the family sessions. If Elena does not take a step, time does not go by; it stops. Her ability to walk and, in a broad sense, her entire development have activated in them fantasies of illness, aging, and death. In addition, stagnation may have also been enhanced by the presence of the grandmother, which has actualized fantasies; what they fear lies in their sight.

As Piera Aulagnier (1989) states, "may nothing change" is a deathly desire. The lack of acceptance of the passage of time requires disavowal. "May nothing change" regarding the bodies of the baby and the grandmother is an impossible wish. Elena is already too big for her crib, and in the case of the grandmother, the distance between her room and the living room has "grown." Unconsciously, the parents have sought shelter in immobility. Freezing time seems to offer them some relief, but the price is high. Perhaps stagnation settled when the girl started leaving the breastfeeding stage behind and making progress in her development – walk, speech, potty training – while the grandmother started regressing – arteriosclerosis and its consequences, immobility, and loss of control.

In the course of the link sessions strong fears also emerged that Elena would get hurt if she walked. The work of the therapeutic companion, therefore, aimed at promoting games that favored movement outside the home. When they went out, the mother would insist on bringing the stroller, and when they reached the park, Elena would refuse to get out. The therapeutic companion suggested that they go without the stroller.

16 Couples and families today

Leaving the stroller behind helped the mother overcome her fear, thus enabling them to play.

Shortly afterward Elena stood up. She was extremely excited when she realized she could hold herself up. From then on, a recurring game started. Elena would stand on the feet of the companion, insisting that the companion move. She would thus start moving her legs and would walk without losing sight of the companion, "supporting herself" on the companion's gaze. When the parents saw her walking, they were both happy and alarmed. In the office they would carefully watch the girl's movements. They slowly incorporated the idea that Elena could move around without getting hurt.

Some time later Elena "set herself in motion." While they were very appreciative, the parents terminated the treatment alluding to financial difficulties. The analyst received a call from the neurologist, who told her that the parents had gone to see him. They were very grateful, and had shown him, joyful and relieved, that their daughter could walk.

This story, taken from clinical practice, faces us with a hard counterpoint between the helplessness of the "setting in motion" of life and the helplessness of its last stages. In healthcare work, giving a new meaning to a way to face difficulties is key. Particularly when dealing with children, like Elena, making room for tumbling as part of their process and evolution is decisive. There is no mobility without falling down; no learning is possible if we do not contemplate error as one of its unavoidable components.

This clinical material shows how building situational networks with engaged, sensitive professionals makes it possible to configure custommade therapeutic devices in a creative way. Link work starts with the first visit and facilitates the use of a variety of tools that help restrain resistances and render suffering more endurable.

Second clinical narrative: an intervention during a crisis

Pedro, aged 19, asks for an urgent family interview, which he attends with his mother and his sister Valeria, aged 22. They seek help after a robbery carried out by Valeria's friends. She had given away copies of the house keys to all her acquaintances. Money and jewelry were taken. Pedro says his sister lies, conceals things, and endangers them. Valeria retorts, "Pedro is perfect. If God exists, his name is Pedro." Pedro points out that if he doesn't take care of things, nothing gets done. "They look the other way." Silvia, the mother doesn't see, or doesn't want to see. The sister takes no responsibility.

Valeria explains that she had to shoulder her father's death on her own – take charge of everything. She was very sick; they had to hospitalize her due to bleeding ulcers. Pedro accuses her of always wanting to attract attention. "She has sixteen piercings in her body and belly," he says, "and even one in the tongue. She takes drugs, she does everything wrong, and the kids who robbed us also took drugs. We made a mistake; we thought that once we moved to this house, things would be different. We wouldn't live with Jorge [the mother's long-time boyfriend] because our attempt to live all together failed. We would have a place for the three of us and would live in peace. But with the robbery everything blew out." Valeria retorts, "If I'm the entire problem, I'll leave, I'll disappear and that's it."

A month after starting treatment Valeria runs away from home and they can't find her. She leaves a note saying that she had tried to commit suicide and was saved by a friend "who is like a soul mate." A year earlier she had already written that her life was useless, that she felt like a scourge, a waste. According to the mother, "Valeria expressed her problems through her body. At one point she weighed one hundred and sixty-five pounds, and at another point, one hundred." The father died in an accident. It was not clear whether it was an accident or a suicide. He was violent; he used to beat Silvia.

The family analysis went on with Silvia and Pedro, and at the analyst's suggestion, Silvia started attending a support group for family members of addicts. In this way, the clinical device was expanded. Also during that time, responding to a request made by Silvia and Jorge, the analyst conducted some couple sessions simultaneously, because the failure of the plan to move all together had created tension in the relationship.

Six months after her disappearance, Valeria announces that she is coming back to Buenos Aires. Upset, Pedro mentions that he was the last one to know but that he's not surprised, because in his family "nobody knows anything about anybody, we operate like islands." And Silvia adds, "When the father was here it was the same way; he allied himself with the kids, but he monopolized them." Hurt, Pedro reacts: "Didn't you realize that I was always at your side? I was the one who stood behind the door to intervene when he beat you." Then he suggests that each family member follow his or her own path, with the idea of dismantling the link device. Family fragmentation might have worsened if a multifaceted device had not been preserved that included Valeria, despite her absence, and the father, the manner of whose death had been uncertain and for whom mourning still seemed to be pending.

Vignette of a session after six months

Silvia: "I found a solution for the problem of meals [she does not like to cook]. Since I noticed that my mom was depressed, I assigned her the task of cooking. Many grandmothers make food for their grandchildren. Now she's happy, she looks for recipes, she feels useful. The kids' dad was a great cook; he would make delicious dishes with a great presentation. Now we can go back to eating tasty food every day, and Pedro is also happy. [They laugh.] On a

18   Couples and families today

different note, I suggested that if Valeria came back, things with her would not be the same as before, but there are also things I want to mention about Pedro. We have to make changes; we have to review everything – order and disorder, money management, expenses. . . . He likes expensive clothes, like his father, but leaves them wet in the washer, and they get ruined."

Pedro: "It's not that I wear expensive clothes. I buy a good pair of jeans, but I only have one, and another one that I can barely wear because it's too tight, and I want to have children. The thing is, I don't care if Valeria comes home, I already decided I'll pay no attention to her; I'll listen to my friends, who tell me that with your family it's best to pretend and not to be so committed. I want to live my life, do my own thing. Last year I almost lost a school year trying to save my sister."

Analyst: "Perhaps you will no longer have to occupy that place that led Valeria to say in the first interview that if there's a God, his name is Pedro."

Silvia: [Laughs.] "How did you remember that? Because his dad also said that."

Analyst: [Surprised] "What did his dad say?"

Silvia: It was a phrase that was commonly used in the family. . . . That if there's a God, his name is so and so, but his dad said that he [the father] was God."

Pedro: "Speaking of which, I always said that if there was something I wanted to be it is a dad."

Some thoughts on the material

It is striking that, as a family, they describe themselves more through their disconnection than through their sense of being a group of belonging. Together, they say, they operate like islands; nobody knows anything about anyone. When they moved to their new place, they envisioned themselves living in peace, without the father and without Jorge. Yet Valeria gives away the house keys indiscriminately, thus producing an uncontrolled openness.

What position does each one take? Pedro denounces and accuses his sister of endangering herself and them, and his mother of not seeing anything. Valeria seems to embody the father's death. With her acts she denounces a void, the lack of support, the inability to separate. Confusion, isolation, and expulsion seem to be the fate of the members of this family.

Family signifiers circulate as dichotomies. The words "everything" and "nothing" pervade the material. There are those who "always attract attention," and others who "always try to look the other way." "Everything is perceived" in the body, or "nothing is perceived." There are those who "take responsibility for everything," and others who "don't take responsibility for anything." They occupy the "taking charge" places successively, one at a time, and they always systematically fail. The omnipotent, violent father has left an empty place. Valeria takes responsibility for "the entire" family until she breaks down, pierces herself, and says, "Enough." Then she needs to vanish. Pedro takes on "the entire" responsibility with unwavering conviction. Finally, it is the mother who, thanks to the analysis, seems to be able to start taking responsibility. Is this the first hint of difference?

To conclude, the presentation of this clinical vignette aims to show how we understand linking practices, and how analysts and patients develop variations in the device over the course of the analysis. Devices are hence situational rather than fixed, and may change depending on immanent rules. Their purpose is to generate spaces of containment, working-through, and support in order to act upon the family crisis. Developing resources and tools is part of our task.

Psychoanalysis as device

An epistemological turn toward complexity has taken place in the last decades that has led to the adoption of the concept of device in psychoanalysis. We no longer see our discipline as closed upon itself. Rather, we see it as a device whose heterogeneous web transcends the theoretical-clinical dimension.

We chose to delve into the Foucauldean concept of device because it alludes to the networks of relationships that can be identified among scientific writing, institutions, and institutional discourses and rules. From a clinical perspective, alert to the manifold interstices of this hinge concept, as Foucault called it, we began to consider the possibility of viewing psychoanalysis itself as a device. In this book, however, we focus on the notion of psychoanalytic device as a tool that can be developed and tailored to address clinical situations. In the following chapters we continue mapping the clinical territory of this conceptualization by discussing a variety of materials drawn from link psychoanalytic practice.

Notes

1 The concept of device derives from the term "dispositif" used originally in French by M. Foucault. Since this author did not object to its English translation as "device," we have adopted his criterion.
2 While in Bleger's book "encuadre" was translated as "frame," the authors have chosen to translate it as "setting."

Chapter 2

The suffering of couples and families

There is no human existence outside the space of links, where subjects are constituted as such. To belong to a link in a specific space and time, subjects must perform the psychic work needed to process difference. Doing something with difference means transforming and renouncing the drive forces at play in relationships. Gomel and Matus (2011, p. 63) define link suffering as "the unavoidable remainder, the unsuturable discrepancy between the psychic work needed for link organization and individual modes of operation."

Suffering is inherent in links; it is part of the libidinal investiture, of the paradox of love, and therefore not necessarily pathological. According to Persia, "we inevitably grieve in the face of illness, death, or lack of love" (Persia, 2012, no pagination). Yet as Persia also states, the fact that it is inevitable does not mean we must be slaves to this pain. In this sense, Bianchi argues that suffering:

> is both a need and a risk. It is a need because it forces subjects to acknowledge the difference between reality and fantasy as well as the differences among themselves. Yet it is also a risk because faced with excess suffering, one may restrict or annul one's relationship with the other through disinvestiture.
>
> (Bianchi, 2005, no pagination)

Illusion is always restored when acknowledgment occurs. In return, disavowal and/or repudiation are at the root of link pathology and cause unnecessary suffering.

Looking at link psychoanalytic practice from the viewpoint of suffering implies devoting ourselves to the alleviation of psychic pain without focusing on psychopathologies or diagnostic classifications, but without dismissing them either. This approach allows us to decenter and deconstruct rigid diagnoses (e.g. the DSM) that freeze subjects in unchangeable categories. Only then shall we be able to analyze the complexity of suffering derived from link conflicts, from unconscious pacts and alliances.

The suffering of couples and families 21

Link construction calls for the intertwining of three dimensions, namely, alienness, sameness, and difference. Establishing links would be impossible without the presence of both the illusion of sameness and the acknowledgment of the other as different. Clinical practice shows that acknowledging differences among subjects facilitates skirting the perception of the ultimate impossibility of links. Patients can thus forge a sublimation path in the link, which will enable them to perceive foreignness (Matus and Moscona, 1995).

While it is true that desiring life is exposed to each subject's singular history, it is also true, as Ritvo, affirms, that we pay a price for living a desiring life, where we are never "safe from our fellow beings' impostures, from our neighbors' cruelty, from the compelling enigma of the Other" (Ritvo, 2012, p. 130). Although the notion of link suffering may induce us to think that all the members of a link suffer in the same way, this is not the case. Suffering is individual. Freud already pointed out that the seat of anxiety is the ego, and stressed that "The suffering which comes from this last source [the others] is perhaps more painful to us than any other" (Freud, 1930, p. 77).

Isn't suffering the chief complaint of subjects, couples, families, groups, and institutions? As we already pointed out, considering that suffering, and the situations that condition it, operates with a link logic involves significant decisions regarding clinical strategy and the choice of a device and an interpretation path. Link psychoanalytic devices promote the creation of new bonds, the emergence of unprecedented experiences that make it possible to find new meanings. We agree with Janine Puget that

> at the theoretical-clinical level, we need interventions that will not only refer to unconscious infantile conflicts, but also focus on the implications of living on quicksand, in other words, on the effects of the present.
>
> (Puget, 2014)

How does suffering operate, and what causes it? In some links, pain is a condition of existence, a condition of jouissance. Suffering is eroticized, and the other is an object of need. These bonds create a vicious cycle. Aulagnier (1980) refers to alienating links, where a desire to alienate the other's desire meets a desire for self-alienation.

The desire to alienate oneself in a passion may operate as a narcissistic defense against the suffering inherent in the work of mourning. In the desire to alienate through passion, in turn, a demand for the narcissistic exaltation of power and mastery is at play. The tendency to forge passionate relationships constitutes both a risk and a temptation for us all, and certain life circumstances (encounters or failed encounters) may trigger it.

22 Couples and families today

The consequences of link suffering refer not only to the loss of love but also to detachment, separation, and link death. In extreme cases, this suffering leaves subjects in a state of emotional defenselessness, disquietude, and even dis-existence. Byung-Chul Han (2015) alludes to the burnout society and the production of exhausted, ghostly subjects who can only act automatically within the parameters of the system. Excess positivity produces, among other things, depression, burnout, attention deficit, panic attacks, hyperconnectivity syndrome, and addictions, indicating the victory of globalized capitalism.

It is often our bodies that display the consequences of this unprocessed suffering. Faced with a shock, they respond in the only way available to them – they become ill. Other times, as we already mentioned, link members are trapped in alienating bonds. They are under the illusion that addictive attachment to the link will give them the yearned-for sense of completion that will relieve the anxiety caused by emptiness.

Lack of recognition and the feeling of not belonging in a link also produce suffering. This is the case of inflexible modalities that tend to crystallize in repetitive scenes, endless fights, recriminations, demands, jealousy, and acts of passionate violence. The "characteropathization" of links, the symptomatic adherence to a deadly mode of functioning prevents movement and metaphoric creation. Transforming suffering into words, carrying out a work of mourning, and not anesthetizing ourselves allow us to transform the unassimilable into symbols.

The obliteration of the other's subjectivity that we find in present-day modes of suffering is associated with impunity and the abuse of power, and the undermining of the symbolic order and desubjectivation are some of its effects. Psychoanalysis is striving to expand the map of significations and open to new forms of psychic causality. A certain faith in the act of listening to the unconscious is present in the analyst-patient interaction that makes it possible to glimpse at the truth and bring some relief to link suffering.

Configurations of suffering: two vignettes on current chief complaints

Nancy and Gustavo live together and plan to get married this year. The psychiatrist who medicates them suggested that they start couple therapy. They met three years ago at a club where drugs were readily available. They started hanging out with a group of friends of Gustavo's who used cocaine. They tried "everything!" Nancy comes from a non-observant Catholic family of Spanish origin. Gustavo, from a very traditional Jewish family. The idea was that Nancy would convert to Judaism before they got married. She started attending courses with a rabbi to prepare for conversion.

The suffering of couples and families   23

Nancy: "I had a very bad week. I asked my analyst for a session. I was choking. I couldn't breathe. I was in a state of crisis that's very difficult to explain. I felt I was about to explode. A freezing cold ran through my entire body. Finally I passed out. Luckily, I was in bed. I can't remember anything of what happened after that."

Gustavo: "I tried to calm her down. I gave her some tips so that she wouldn't be so upset. It happens to me too, and I can overcome it with some techniques."

Nancy: "You're not dealing with what I'm dealing with. . . . Even though my family is not religious and they don't say anything, I've been feeling like a traitor. I remembered when I used to go to church with my grandmother. . . . I decided to convert because it's important to him, and also because I like what I've learned about Judaism. It seems interesting to me in terms of our children's education."

Gustavo: "We've talked about this since the beginning of the relationship, and it was agreed."

It is difficult for this couple to create a converging space, a "we." They take for granted that only one of them needs to change. Nancy should abandon, "let go" of her religion and even her culture, and Gustavo is the one who lays down the law. Perhaps a goal of their analysis should be to engage in a reciprocal transformation. To this end, they would have to reformulate their unconscious pacts and agreements in order to build something new and unprecedented for both of them.

In other sessions Nancy complains that her partner wants to educate her because "she's a brat and was spoiled by her family, she's not used to sharing," nor to giving something up for the sake of the link. Sometimes, love, power, and mastery relations combine with a need to make the otherness of the other disappear and to transform the two into one.

Sofia and Federico, 24 and 26 years old

Federico: "We met through an Internet website. I had ended a relationship of several years with a high school sweetheart, and my friends advised me to use Tinder or Happen to date women and have a good time with no strings attached. That way I wouldn't feel down anymore. I went out with several girls but didn't hook up with any of them. I abandoned the game. I thought it was a waste of time, and it bored me. Since I speak Italian, I signed up to a website to practice the language. That's how I met Sofia, who happened to be from Argentina. We had chemistry, and we also hit it off. Our relationship lasted three months on Skype."

24 Couples and families today

Sofia: "I was doing an architecture internship in Florence, and I had fun talking to Federico. He was amusing, and I felt a bit lonely in Europe."

Federico: "We Skyped every day for one or two hours. We talked about our everyday lives but also about serious stuff related to our respective love lives, our lives in general, our family and friends. I live alone, and I showed her my house via Skype. A real tour [they laugh]."

Sofia: "I realized I couldn't wait to talk to Federico, to the point that I started to get scared. What if the whole thing was crazy, and when we met, everything ended up being a great disappointment, the product of an absurd fantasy?"

Federico: "I had the same fears, but I didn't tell Sofia. I was happy to connect and share that time with her."

Sofia: "When I finished my internship and was about to go back to Buenos Aires, I started getting anxious about what would happen when we saw each other in person, when we touched and kissed."

Federico: "Well, it wasn't that dramatic, but some things started happening to us that weren't happening during our Skype stage. And now we're here to consult with you."

Analyst: "What things started happening when you met?"

Sofia: "One is that he gets upset because, according to him, I'm looking at my cell phone all the time to connect with my friends. I discovered that he's very jealous, more than I'd thought! I have to tell him everything I do, when before I just turned the computer on and off with a simple click. The way he eats and the noises he makes bother me. It's as if some of the magic had been lost, and we're no longer who we thought we were."

Federico: "But, then, do you think we made up an image of someone we're not through the Internet?"

Sofia: "I don't know. It's not clear to me, and I don't know how to explain it, but something changed, transformed, or was lost."

The other's actual presence demands that they work against idealization and the projecting tendencies that the virtual world may promote and/or stimulate. The Internet offers spaces where subjects can unfold their fantasies. We lie with the truth. We believe we are in front of real life when we are actually in front of a fiction (Sahovaler de Litvinoff, 2009). Is it possible to go beyond online passion? Virtual reality tends to erase the impositions of real life, and the idea that everything is possible is reinforced.

Concluding thoughts

The link perspective has brought about a shift in psychoanalytic theory, and hence in clinical work, because its object of study is the subject of the unconscious as a subject of the link. The goal is to work with what takes place in the present of the session in the presence of the subjects of the link. Conflicts and misunderstandings develop among participants in the link, who forge unconscious alliances to repress and/or disavow in order to mitigate suffering.

Subjects aim to protect themselves by symptomatically avoiding anxiety (Freud, 1926). Symptoms will depend on their repertory of symbolic resources and on the culture where they are inscribed. Different historical and cultural contexts foster different ways of negotiating and processing anxiety. A culture that seeks to eradicate anxiety tends toward the proliferation of symptoms, which result from subjects' efforts to stifle their pain.

When conflict appears, subjects become their own spokespeople. They produce new meanings to cope with anxiety. Theirs is a "subjectivity in production." The fixity and stereotypy of the symptom go against the moving forces of conflict. The symptom takes over the subject; it is the foreign that imposes its presence. It corresponds to that aspect of the subject that is congealed, that bogs down.

A state of openness to the encounter enables analysts and patients to jointly create a unique situational device for each case. According to Jullien (2013), availability is a working concept that refers to a position without position. In this way, analysts can grasp, focus on, and sustain different possibilities simultaneously. Availability involves maintaining an open range of options, a kind of "hospitality of devices" to address current suffering.

The clinical device is designed step by step. It is a process of "progressively doing" in the immanence of the session, and requires that we assess the need to intervene based on current circumstances. Our interventions will be validated a posteriori. Analysis can only happen if there is a state of availability. The use of diverse situational psychoanalytic devices allows us to work with new tools while respecting the Freudian legacy of an unconscious that develops gradually and situationally in the transference.

Chapter 3

Family practice

Ana and Arturo seek help for their son Darío, aged 17. They would like him to start treatment, even though they know it is unlikely that he will agree to come to the office. They have a 13-year-old daughter, Ariana, who has a mental disability due to having suffered anoxia during her birth. Ariana only communicates through gestures and sounds. She is a loving girl, and actively interacts with her family despite her disability. She attends a full-day special education school.

Ana and Arturo are very pleasant. There is no perceptible tension in their relationship. Both seem very distressed about their eldest son, who left home after a year of constant fighting. They believe he moved in with his friend Gabriel, who came to Buenos Aires from the provinces and is two years Darío's senior. Things changed during the last year. At a certain point Gabriel had practically moved in. Ana and Arturo had the same reaction to this development: "We felt we were living in a squat."

Gabriel is a professional tennis player. His parents emancipated him before he moved to Buenos Aires so that he would be free to travel whenever the opportunity arose. What follows is Ana's account during the first interview.

> The problem started a few months ago – six or eight. It took us by surprise. Darío changed all of a sudden. He stopped hanging out with his usual friends and started criticizing them. He only wanted to be with Gabriel. Some nights he wouldn't come home. He has also changed how he dresses and the food he eats. The change was, and is, very abrupt. Darío seems like a completely different person. We think he may be into something weird.

Weird alludes to something that is foreign to the family's habits. The parents' imaginary includes the possibility that Darío may have joined a sect. Arturo adds that they thought of having him followed. They fear his life may be in danger.

Ana continues with her narrative:

> We also thought he might be romantically involved with Gabriel. When Gabriel moved in last year, the atmosphere changed. It was hell. They would cook at any time of day. They banged doors. Gabriel walked in front of us as if we weren't there. He wouldn't say hello. It was a mess. Suddenly our son had become a stranger. Still, we didn't want to go on vacation only with Ariana. We insisted that he come because in truth, the good times happen when he's around. In the end he came only for a few days but spent them locked in his room. He never ate with us; he wouldn't talk to us.

When they came back, Gabriel came back as well. His intrusive presence and their uneasy interaction increased the atmosphere of tension. Finally they denied him entrance to the house. Darío got angry, became violent, and a few days later decided to leave. Arturo adds that some money went missing (Ana cries). Arturo says, "We think he's living with Gabriel. He doesn't answer his cell phone. Sometimes he texts back. He only comes home to get money. He also said to us, 'Don't send the police because I'll leave again.' He says he's looking into getting emancipated." Ana adds, "Darío upset the applecart. He left. He knows we're dying, especially me. I'm terrified that something will happen to him."

In view of Darío's obvious absence from the therapeutic framework, the analyst suggests working on the parent-child relationship with the available device. They will have to "cross uncharted territories" to unravel a conflict that has become inaccessible to the family.

During the first sessions the parents discuss different options: bringing him home by force, hiring a detective to follow him, having a juvenile court judge intervene, having Gabriel's family investigated through a contact in the police. Puzzlement, suspicion, and mistrust permeate the atmosphere. Throughout the conversation Ana and Arturo's prejudices emerge. Where there is emancipation there is delinquency; what remains outside the traditional framework is "scum." In this family differentiating oneself means turning into a stranger, and foreign is analogous to dangerous. Difference poses a threat.

Work during the sessions focused on the need to think before making decisions. The analyst's idea was that the device that had been developed could, in principle, curb the escalation of violence. After discussing them in the sessions, Ana and Arturo gave up the manifold alternatives they had considered.

Anxious, mistrustful, overwhelmed, the parents would repeatedly phone the analyst because they could not wait for their hour. They did not know what to do to connect with their son. One afternoon they called

28 Couples and families today

the analyst six times in two hours. After a month-long absence Darío had called his father to say he would come over to get money. The parents' request to the analyst was pressing. They needed an answer. What should they do when Darío came over? They feared that giving him money meant validating his way of life, and not doing so meant leaving him to his own devices.

Since she understood that the parents needed some kind of answer from her, the analyst told them that when Darío arrived they should use only the first person plural: "We have a problem; we're very worried about what's happening to us." She also suggested telling him that they had consulted with an analyst.

This type of intervention tends to be spontaneous, and is generally forced upon the analyst when treating links characterized by the prevalence of discharge and impulsive acts. In this case, the intervention, which took place in the analyst's ten-minute break between patients, had unexpected effects – not only on Darío, who was surprised by his parents' response, but also on Ana and Arturo. In the next session they related that they had started wondering what had happened to them. Something dawned on them that seemed obvious but that they had not been able to consider before: this was not just Darío's problem.

A painful inquiry was opened. The phrase "In truth, the good times happen when he's around" became a key that allowed patients and analyst to delve into the family conflict. Ideas and thoughts formed in relation to this phrase that shed light on dark areas. Ana and Arturo were utterly unaware of the effort Darío had to make to satisfy them and make up for his sister's disability. Ana remembered and brought to the session a letter Darío had written to them months earlier telling them about his personal crisis – about his desire and need to choose what he wanted to do with his life. In the letter Darío complained about the mother's excessive control and the father's absence, and about the fact that they did not encourage his sister to develop a more independent behavior.

Neither Ana nor Arturo understood why they had minimized and later forgotten the content of this letter. Darío had to disappear from his parents' gaze for them to notice him. It was a friend, a peer who supported his separation. His sister, with whom he had a close, warm relationship, was clearly not in a position to help him embark on this journey toward the outside. Darío was able to make explicit the anxiety and ambivalence caused by thinking that he would be in charge of her when his parents were no longer around.

Furthermore, over time, the existence of an implicit agreement between the parents emerged in the sessions. They had divided their children between them. For Ana, Darío's absence was unbearable. "Seeing him makes my day," she stated, "even if he doesn't talk to me; seeing him is enough. The problem is when he's not around." Ana had already expressed this clearly in earlier sessions. "Without Darío we're dying," she had said. Her son was responsible for breathing life into his mother. He sought to make up for the suffering caused by his sister's disability, and also for the emotional distance between Ana and her husband. Having resigned himself to his father's coldness toward him, Darío found shelter in his bond with his mother.

Yet something had altered these long-established dynamics; in the midst of his adolescent crisis, Darío wanted to break away from his mother. Confrontation was Darío's singular way of making himself heard. Both securing emancipation and choosing to become a speech therapist became confrontational vindications. His was a twofold provocation. He was an activist of the "emancipation cause," to his mother's astonishment, and he boasted his interest in speech therapy in front of a father for whom this choice was not a respectable option. In this family anything new was resisted. Family members rejected events because they experienced them as an untimely, violent irruption.

The therapeutic device worked despite Darío's absence. He knew he was invited to participate, and every now and then would ask Ana and Arturo if they were still in treatment. The relationship between parents and child slowly changed. Darío gradually renewed contact with his family. At first he only communicated with his father. Though it was hard for her, Ana tolerated his silence, while Arturo agreed to play a more significant role in his son's life. Still, Darío did not take part in any family activity. His need to bring about a break was clear.

Little by little, the atmosphere became more relaxed. Gabriel came back to visit but did not move in. His occasional presence between trips, which symbolized the ability to envision life as movement in contrast with the family's immobility, was received differently. At the same time, Darío no longer needed his friend as a safe-conduct toward emancipation.

Throughout the ten months of the treatment the parents underwent moments of intense pain. Gradually, they were able to come to terms with their ambivalence and guilt in relation to their children. They also referred to their difficulty to communicate within the couple link. Ana and Arturo were now working to find a different way of offering a home to their children.

Darío's crisis erupted simultaneously with his sister's puberty. Despite having reached this life stage, Ariana was still being fed, cleaned, and treated as if she were a baby, particularly with regard to her relationship with her own body. Through his acts, Darío was including a thirdness, that is, imposing a presence that might neutralize the strong impact of his sister's disability. Perhaps he was also seeking to instate modesty rules appropriate to his and Ariana's age.

As the summer approached, Darío suggested that they vacation at the same beach as his friends. The family was willing to go to the new place.

Coincidentally, the parents suggested ending the treatment. When they left, they stated: "We will stop for now. For now we can continue on our own."

The urgency of clinical demands often leads us to react with some haste. The occasionally pressing need to respond prevents us from carefully studying different options. Emphasizing and insisting on the urgency factor prevents the potential emergence of self-reproach in relation to the constitution of our devices. It becomes necessary, therefore, to distinguish between the creation of a device as a response to an urgent demand, and the joint construction of a device once the urgent situation has been left behind and it is deemed necessary to continue with the treatment.

Once again, conceptualizations derive from the needs suggested by the demands of clinical practice. Along with J.-B. Pontalis, we believe that "clinical experience is the source of thought. . . . Clinical experience contradicts, creates flux, and makes any prefabricated theory vacillate, beginning with our own" (Pontalis, 2003, p. 10). That is how we change with the times – by finding new concepts to respond to the vicissitudes of our practice.

Chapter 4

Couples in conflict

In psychoanalysis, the concept of psychic reality signals the expansion of the boundaries of rationalism thanks to Freud's introduction of the postulate that unconscious reasons have a value of their own. The expression "psychic reality" is controversial in itself. It is a compound formulation whose terms maintain a paradoxical relationship. If *realitas* is the thing "that which is there," "that which is objective," why did Freud postulate its inextricable link to the inaccessible aspects of the psyche, which can only be grasped through their productions and effects?

A look at the context in which these ideas were developed may guide us in venturing some conjectures. Freud's initial theoretical conception was tied to the theory of trauma, which affirmed the existence of the trauma as an undisputable event. The failure of this theory led him to turn to the concept of fantasy and the resulting postulation of the existence of a psychic reality.

As a man of science, Freud espoused rationalist ideals; he believed that there is science if there is a discernible system of laws. Yet he did not hesitate to posit the existence of another reality, a dissonant reality that does not aspire to maintain a correspondence with the reality of the object or to be subjected to the constant testing of its "truth." It is a reality that cannot be encompassed by conscious reasoning. Freud thus reintroduces into the heart of a culture aiming for homogeneity the idea that conflict and psychic splitting are constitutive of human mental functioning and that there is no possible synthesis that will relieve existential tension.

This break with the illusion of a unified subject, of a synthesizing psyche gives rise to the notion of the coexistence of manifold psychic realities, both within each subject and in subjects' significant links. The work of unveiling, resignification, production, and construction that takes place in the analytic process is directed toward recognizing rather than erasing such multiplicity. Subjects never fully renounce the illusion of narcissistic completion. Their quest, however, is destined to fail, because the idea of a totalizing unity is fictitious.

32 Couples and families today

Psychic life is driven by an interface of conflicting forces. Every symptom reveals the splitting to which subjects would rather remain oblivious. The definition of the psychoanalytic field starts with the recognition of subjects as divided between what they say and what remains outside their saying. Moreover, the topographic split is constitutive of the psychic apparatus. The idea of a unitary ego disappears. An attempt emerges to define the ego as conflict, as something that cannot be reduced to a content devoid of tension and dissonance. At the same time, modern literature reflects cultural changes in the conception of the subject. "I is other," claims Rimbaud – several others successively or simultaneously. Dostoyevsky's novel *The Double*, in turn, is a paradigmatic example of the way in which subjects are divided and multiplied in a psychic plurality where each one is other in relation to oneself.

We are used to thinking of splitting as equivalent to dislocation. From the perspective of complexity, how can we envision a working-through that supports and highlights diversity and/or splitting? When we refer to historicization, we allude to links that do not necessarily imply harmony, let alone an interaction free of conflict.

Sonia and Juan are architects, and each has two children from a previous marriage. They have lived together, with their four children, for a few years. Juan contacted the therapist. They need guidance. One of the motivations to seek help is their children, primarily Juan's eldest daughter. "Another issue," adds Juan, "is that we have different sensibilities. I am worldlier; spirituality has little room in my life. I may have 20% of spirituality. Sonia, instead, is 10% worldly and 90% spiritual. She sees, feels, and suffers in a space that is very hard to accept as reality. . . . Tell the therapist the things that happen to you." Upon Juan's insistence, Sonia says, "Well, yes, I see, feel, smell things that most people don't feel, see, or smell. And I perceive the intention to create tension."

Juan: "Yes, because for example, the girl brings something home, and Sonia touches it and suddenly becomes pale, or we're at the table and she starts yawning and can't stop, and she says that there's a negative energy, or, for example, I leave some clothes and she washes them. . . . Tell the therapist why you wash them."

Sonia: "Well, yes. . . . I wash them because I see that those clothes have negative things, things that need to be removed. Why does it bother you that I wash your clothes?"

The fights between Juan and Sonia are very violent. It gradually becomes clear that, faced with Sonia's delirious ideas, which are expressed at times in a very anxious, at times violent way, Juan shows an ambivalent attitude. Sometimes he hesitates. Is it that she is spiritual and he is worldly? Does black magic exist? Is it actually true that if you take pictures in a special way, you will be able to see people's aura and read their future? His doubts cause him to begin by encouraging Sonia to display her "beliefs," and then condemn her and accuse her of being crazy.

Juan draws a line where his children are concerned. Sonia's "beliefs" include the idea that his eldest daughter brings invisible fluids at her mother's request and "dirties" their house. Juan's disavowal drives Sonia to lose control. She screams, swears, cries, threatens. It is a psychotic productivity in which Juan is involved through the link: "Just in case, I want to play both sides."

Sonia accepted neither the therapeutic prescription of individual psychoanalytic treatment nor a referral for psychiatric evaluation, although her clinical picture required this. She maintained her certainties by means of armor consisting of extreme defense mechanisms. In this patient, delusional ideas were associated with spiritualistic practices. The patient's active participation in a group sharing her beliefs provided her with transitional, prosthetic anaclisis. Belonging to this group could help her "socialize her delirium." The establishment of these social ties enabled Sonia to go out into the world around her. Juan, for his part, asked to be referred to a therapist for individual treatment.

In this clinical narrative we see a way of functioning unfold that shows moments of psychotic production (Gomel and Matus, 2011). At the same time, the analytic process with couples requires that we create and recreate the unexpected, that is, an environment where neurotic, perverse, and/or psychotic realities can be displayed and constructed. A transference script should be developed so that analyst and patients can attempt to put together new versions of the patients' history. In this sense, Kaës (2007) suggests thinking of a new metapsychology, a third topography that will account for the intersubjective unconscious. This author believes that psychic reality is both singular and plural.

We need to expand the boundaries of our epistemological references. Complex thought enables us to conceive of the existence of different realities. That is why we agree with Puget (2013) when she argues that the analytic experience cannot generate meaning if we view links and social realities as metaphors for the internal world and this world, insofar as it is internal, as protected from the effects of the present.

Berenstein and Puget have coined a term, *the Two*, that alludes to the radical difference between two or more subjects. They state that in families and couples, similarity and difference intertwine and coexist in that asymptotic difference between subjects marked by alienness/alterity. Links, claims Berenstein (2001), lay the foundations for a different ethics, an ethics that requires that we take into account the other's alien aspects. Subjects must include the other as foreign and hence as not inscribed in the ego.

Recognizing alterity entails acknowledging both the others' and one's own alienness. Analysts who adopt link theory incorporate the

34 Couples and families today

coexistence of different logics into our work. Absence-presence, representation-presentation, history-event, unfolding-production, association-connectivity, transcendence-immanence, Chronos-Aion are pairs of concepts that are traditionally presented as antagonistic. Nonetheless, from the perspective of complexity, they can be approached as based on simultaneous, multiple, and diverse logics. As we have mentioned before, the theories of internal conflict, on the one hand, and of intersubjectivity, on the other refer to different modes of operation that are present in each situation, legalities that interrelate and also enjoy a relative autonomy.

We can define link realities as psychic constructions that emerge from the contingency of singular encounters, of reciprocally significant investitures. They show their effectiveness in the particular positions from where link subjects act in this space and in the specific ways in which they invest it. We are referring to inter-phantasmatic productions that, as described by Spivacow (2005), derive from the unconscious assembly they configure and transcend the sum of the fantasies of both subjects. It is a virtual space with its own laws, which influence, mobilize, and bring this unique relationship to life. Subjectivity and link are simultaneously and mutually configured.

The various link realities interweave discourses. Associative and connective webs and wefts facilitate access to forgotten, minimized, or split scenes and meanings that rarely appear in the association process of an isolated subject. Link psychic reality, which corresponds to a group (a couple or a family), is different and unique for each group member. Link scenes emerge as a plot supported by a multiplicity of presences and representations that will give rise to new productions. It is an immanent work.

The so-called *subjects of the link* create situations, atmospheres, and experiences in the link that leave traces, marks that can be either reparatory or toxic and alienating. The following clinical vignette illustrates the difficulties that emerge when the unconscious alliances that structure the couple link are brought to a crisis.

Gustavo: "I think Elena is in really bad shape. If she's in bad shape, I can't be well. I wrote a poem: 'Elena and Gustavo walk hand in hand, open the gates of heaven, and God joyfully watches the meeting of two soul mates.' I need Elena to be well."

Elena: "I'm still mad at life; it destroyed me, I have no energy. When Gustavo got sick, I changed a lot of things. I don't want him to get so upset about old stories. That's why I think you have to like it or lump it. There are many stories. I don't say anything, and swallow my spite."

Gustavo: "Elena is talking about the conflicts with my siblings, but she also has conflicts with her profession because she doesn't feel fulfilled. And she gets angry with me because she says I always want to be right."

Elena:	"We don't agree, we have different opinions about almost everything. With the kids, Gustavo is more lenient and I'm more demanding."
Gustavo:	"I don't think I'm a good father. I don't take everything into account; I have a hard time setting boundaries."
Elena:	"I have a hard time letting go. Gustavo's siblings take advantage of him, especially one of them. I point it out to him, but he lets it pass."
Gustavo:	"We had a lot of issues with Elena because of this. That's why I decided to have as little contact with my siblings as possible. I favored my marriage. She's very jealous of my siblings. I used to get together with my brother and my cousin every Wednesday, and I had to stop going. Now I only work with them. We're doing great."
Elena:	"I think Gustavo got sick after a bad row with his brother."
Gustavo:	"A few minutes ago, when I was thinking about the last session while I waited for Elena at the corner coffee shop, I had the idea of drawing both the history of our relationship and how I see it today, and bring the drawing here. Now we're two circles in one; we've blended."
Elena:	"He says we've blended. That's how I see all couples – the two people together in the same circle. If one leaves the circle, the couple no longer exists. The greater the distance, the greater the problems, and then they break up." (See Figures 4.1 and 4.2.)

This material shows the constituting paradox experienced by a couple, whose members simultaneously strive toward fusion (the need to create a link) and toward discrimination and difference (which are indispensable for growth). It is likely that the significant losses suffered by both partners during the first years of their relationship (Gustavo's parents died a few months apart, and Elena lost a younger brother) contributed to the development of an unconditional, indissoluble alliance that hindered discrimination and the reformulation of pacts and agreements. In the first interview Elena recalls how Gustavo "would pick me up every Sunday to go to the cemetery."

Survivors of a catastrophe, they were bound by a constitutive alliance of support that promoted the fixity of investitures and fed their narcissistic illusion of completeness. Establishing an absorbing bond, adopting a possessive, clinging attitude and sustaining the illusion of being one with the other as the prevailing quality of the link helped them face successive traumas. It was a way of keeping afloat in the midst of a devastating situation. Gustavo's graphic production appears over the course of the couple therapy as an expression of the inescapable need to review the fixity of those covenants that ensured the link at one time but jeopardize it today. Something began to shift and aroused anxiety and resistance.

Figure 4.1 Our couple at the beginning

As René Kaës suggests,

> these two points relate dialogically: clinical practice warns us that any change in the alliance, for example, the agreements and pacts that are the basis of the shared and common psychic reality, undermines the unconscious psychic structure of every subject. In turn, any change in the structure, economy or dynamic, of the subject,

Couples in conflict 37

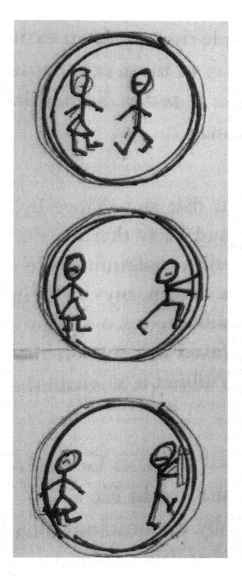

Figure 4.2 Our couple now

(e.g. a therapy, a divorce, adolescent years), clashes with the forces that support the alliances established in the link, in which the subject is an established part.

(Kaës, 2004, no pagination)

38 Couples and families today

This process is reflected both in Gustavo's drawings and in the resistances his testimony aroused in Elena.

The link is supported by unconscious alliances that ensure a certain stability. Crisis situations drive patients to seek help. In some cases, they are able to reformulate the founding pacts and agreements; in others, a breakup is the outcome. It is also common for health professionals to refer couples to therapy as a response to patients' suffering due to the sudden appearance of a psychic or somatic disorder.

Kaës defines unconscious alliances as

> intersubjective psychic formations created by the subjects of a link to reinforce . . . some processes, functions, or structures resulting from repression or disavowal. These formations offer link members such a benefit that the link that bonds them acquires a decisive value for their psychic lives. . . . The idea of unconscious alliance involves an obligation and a dependence.
>
> (Kaës, 1999, p. 113)

Such alliances reveal that links are not random and that they are governed by rules that interpret reality in a biased, singular way.

This author distinguishes three major categories of alliances, namely, structuring, defensive, and offensive alliances. The first ones are "complementary, solidary, and synergic." They are established on the basis of the Oedipal contract with the symbolized father, the fraternal pact, incest prohibition, the renunciation of the direct realization of destructive drive aims, and the narcissistic contract as defined by Piera Aulagnier.

Defensive alliances, in turn, are tied to what has been negativized in the link and are closely related to the notion of denial pact. This pact consists in the "various operations (repression, disavowal, repudiation) required from subjects in every intersubjective link for the link to develop and persist," and it "supports the illusion that the link mocks radical negativity . . ., which refers to the irreducible 'unbound'" (Kaës, 1991, p. 6). Besides being necessary for its establishment, the denial pact creates areas of silence in the link that cannot be signified or transformed. These areas render subjects oblivious to their own history. As to offensive alliances, they are sealed through an agreement to attack or impose. The psychopathic alliance is a case in point.

Thinking about link realities involves being alert to the agreements and pacts that are present in each link, since these constitute the raw matter of unconscious alliances. In some links, agreements and pacts may respond to the variations and movements taking place over the course of patients' lives and of the therapy. In families and couples, different evolving realities coexist and overlap: the reality of the couple's link, of the bonds between each couple member and each child, of the links between siblings, and of the partners' relationship with the families of origin and with their environment. We are faced with a "dissimilar set" that forms an unstable combination (Gomel, 1976).

Beatriz requested an urgent couple interview. She came alone; her partner could not come. She told the therapist that they had already decided to have an abortion. Beatriz was 45 and had no children. Julio was 55 and had two children from a previous marriage. They had lived together for eight years. They got along really well, she said. They traveled, wrote, and were at peace with the idea of not having kids. "Children don't move me." "I'm more than happy with my three nieces." She was thrilled with her new job, which she had wanted for a long time and was not willing to lose.

"Our life project doesn't include motherhood, but I got pregnant, so we decided to terminate the pregnancy," she said, and her tone sounded like a warning to the therapist that this decision would not be reconsidered. They had already seen the gynecologist, who had referred them to a doctor who would perform the abortion. The date had been set. Moreover, she stressed that getting the doctor's number had been a relief.

Somewhat surprised, the analyst wondered why Beatriz had come, especially considering that the person who had referred her was a former patient whom the analyst had helped primarily with her motherhood. Beatriz set clear boundaries to her consultation: "We come to find help to cope with the abortion – at least, to be prepared for this predicament."

Both partners showed up for the second interview, as Beatriz had anticipated. Julio said he liked the idea of thinking things over together so that they could be better equipped to face the problem. He spoke about his fears, about the inadvisability of being a father-grandfather (wondering if it would be healthy), and about his limited ability to bring up a child at this stage in his life. He spoke very affectionately, and said he was willing to go along with his wife's decision, whatever it was. He added that they did not use contraception because the gynecologist had assured Beatriz that she could not get pregnant due to an endocrine dysfunction. At a certain point, far into the interview, the analyst asked, "Did a sperm cell, or perhaps some ambivalence, slip through?"

They did not show up for the next interview; Julio had developed an arrhythmia, and he needed to undergo some tests that had upset their calendar. The analyst thought they would never come back. Yet they came a few weeks later, with some news. "A change of plans slipped through," they said. They had decided to go ahead with the pregnancy and had canceled their appointment with the doctor who was going to perform the abortion. In that session they were able to speak about their fantasies, to envision something of the vital change they were affecting.

Another example: two women, Mónica and Sandra, got married and decided to have a child. They resorted to a homemade insemination with sperm donated by a friend. This friend and his male partner remained

40 Couples and families today

emotionally linked to the child, Vicente, whom they visited regularly. Mónica and Sandra's marriage ended due to unresolvable misunderstandings. Mónica kept the child, whom she had borne, and Sandra was left out of the family scene. Feeling desperate, Sandra sought help. She asked for "a space to think" because her relationship with Vicente was threatened. She fought relentlessly to get a visiting schedule so that she could maintain and regulate her contact with her son.

These reflections on clinical practice emerged from pondering the many modes of presentation of couple consultations. In link interventions, we focus on the ways in which individual and link modes of functioning develop and interact. A dynamic clinical practice depends on a smooth interaction between the cultural and social dimensions of life, on one side, and the nature of our professional interventions, on the other. A "transitional" clinical practice working on links takes into account contextual implications and effects, the circumstances of the parental couple, and unconscious motivations and determinations.

Such a practice constitutes a space where moments of development are challenged, where fantasized representations concerning the families of origin are questioned or revisited. It explores the aspects of the unconscious that pose obstacles, or aims to inscribe the new that has not achieved representation to date. Gauging the scope of a problem is critical in more than one sense. We believe that the way we position ourselves before a conflict is part of the problem, that is, helps configure it. Once the conflict has been identified, we need to determine the potential for working-through (Mauer and May, 2012). The next vignette illustrates the difficulties that may arise when the subjects who are trying to create a link are clinging to pacts and agreements established in their families of origin.

Lorena and Ernesto are young professionals who got married three years ago. They are both undergoing individual psychotherapy. They seek help at the suggestion of their respective therapists because a repetitive circularity has emerged in their personal analyses. They engage in recurring arguments and verbal aggression, and their suffering is great. They claim they love each other, but they both vehemently defend a personal position that refers them to their respective family history and culture, hence the fierce confrontation that has brought them to a link therapy.

Lorena argues that Ernesto forces her to carry out certain religious practices that he considers "unwaiverable," such as attending mass, praying before eating, and dressing modestly. Ernesto claims that Lorena, who strives to be submissive and complaisant with everyone, especially with her parents and siblings, is spiteful and challenging with him. She fights with him about everything, never admits that he is right, and does not satisfy any of his requests.

Ernesto belongs to a very conservative Catholic family. He was educated in religious schools and brought up in a very closed community.

Moreover, he works for the family business. He says he is proud of his family and of the education he received. In his narrative, he underscores that there were no divorces in his family, and adds that his parents and siblings always welcomed Lorena. Contrariwise, he feels that his in-laws have systematically excluded him in different ways. Lorena, by contrast, belongs to an allegedly very "open" family, where new couples have formed after separations. Her parents, recently divorced, relate to her as if she were still single, ignoring her husband. She offers no resistance to this behavior; rather, it seems to please her. The one who finds it extremely upsetting is Ernesto.

Ernesto and Lorena's life together is fraught with conflict that affects their ability to develop a shared life project. Each one feels that the other wants to impose his or her way of doing things, style, and habits, a feeling that results in strong resistances to linking.[1] When they got married, they believed that loving one another meant that they would agree on everything and wish for the same things. The inevitable irruption of difference destroyed this expectation. In the face of the psychic pain derived from their frustration, both tried to entrench themselves defensively in their own psychic reality, populated with well-known family marks.

Analytic work has allowed them to review and process their subjective positioning. Their certainties have gradually become more flexible, and they are able to make room for the other and accept their own alienness. They have slowly built a linking reality they can inhabit and have been able to enter into new pacts and agreements. These changes are evinced in their current relationship with their families of origin and in how they position themselves regarding the other. Their new linking reality has motivated them to want to have a child and form a family with its own rules. Their fantasies feed off and intertwine with each other.

Unmasking and taking apart repetition circuits facilitates the resolution of suffering and malaise. The power of the encounter results from subjects' surrendering and opening to the vicissitudes of life in the immanence of the session. The alliances that participate in this unique configuration are unconscious and produce unconsciousness. The influence of the imponderable and the role of uncertainty make us think that history does not have the last word. Significant encounters inscribe new realities, thus generating a possible space for the unexpected.

Note

1 Concept alluding to different forms of clinical expression that unfold throughout the analysis as a consequence of unconsciously negating, disavowing, or repudiating those elements that mark subjects as *subjects of the link* (Krakov, 1988).

Chapter 5

Thinking about siblings

Life always surprises us. The arrival of a sibling is one of the first strong shocks that challenge us to grow. Making room for a new member of the family, learning to tolerate jealousy, learning to live in harmony with others, all these requirements render the fraternal bond into a complex domain that neither gives respite nor offers alternatives. Parity confronts us with unique challenges. Early bonds between siblings will result in the presence or absence of values that are crucial to our life with others.

Siblinghood is the paradigm of horizontal ties. A range of seemingly irreconcilable emotions converge in the fraternal link. When referring to this moment of family metamorphosis, Freud states: "When other children appear on the scene the Oedipus complex is enlarged into a family complex" (Freud, 1916–17, pp. 333–334).

The arrival of a sibling awakens intense feelings – jealousy, rage, and fear of being displaced. Jealousy stems from the Oedipus or "brother-and-sister complex," as Freud called it (Freud, 1922, p. 223). Lacan (1988) specifically refers to an "intrusion complex" to denote the experience undergone by the child when a new sibling arrives. This complex will trigger different reactions depending on whether it appears before or after the Oedipus complex.

The sibling is perceived as an intruder, a foreigner, and, simultaneously, as someone who is similar and shares the same family. The tension between resemblance and difference is inherent in the fraternal link. An unyielding quest for differentiation and an irreducible yearning for homogeneity play an important role in fraternity. A broad array of fraternal linking configurations ranges from the impulse to fuse, to fratricidal hatred (Assoun, 2000).

Rafael Novoa's brief story (2002, no pagination) serves as eloquent illustration of this process:

> I never forgave my twin brother for leaving me alone in Mom's belly for seven minutes.... These ... [seven minutes] eventually determined

that he would be the eldest and mom's favorite. Since then I always left every place before Paul. . . . One day I got distracted and my brother went outside first, and as he looked at me with that lovely smile, he was run over by a car.

I remember my mother . . . running past me, screaming my name with arms outstretched toward my brother's dead body. I never corrected her mistake.

Failures both in the constitution of the ego and in the link between siblings may suggest a traumatic structuring of subjectivity. Freud ascribed a decisive influence to the fraternal complex. He wrote to his friend Fliess in 1897 that the early death of his brother Julius at nine months (when Sigmund was less than two years old) had sowed in him the seed of self-reproach because he had greeted that brother with "adverse wishes and genuine childhood jealousy" (Masson, 1985, p. 268).

Furthermore, in a letter to Thomas Mann written when he was almost at the end of his life, Freud (1970) surprises us with his analysis of Napoleon. He wonders if the life of Joseph, the biblical character, could have served as a mythical prototype for the French emperor, as the name of his elder brother was Joseph. The desire to eliminate his brother, to take his place, and even to become Joseph may have been the emotion that drove Napoleon's conquests. Freud wonders (p. 433): "Where else could one go but Egypt if one were Joseph and wanted to loom large in the brothers' eyes?"

According to Freud, Napoleon's passion for Egypt attests to the fact that his brother provided the signifier for idealization and aggressiveness. Napoleon conquered Egypt and settled his brothers at the four corners of his empire. Moreover, he chose a wife named Josephine, a name that enabled him to transfer to her part of the tender attachment he had felt for his elder brother. When he repudiates Josephine, thus displacing onto her his hostility toward Joseph, Napoleon's decline begins, ultimately leading to his downfall. Freud's account of Napoleon's history allows him to interpret that the conqueror's defeat resulted from self-punishment for both his betrayal of Josephine and his destructive fraternal impulses.

The fraternal complex

There are two reasons for our interest in the fraternal link. First, in our clinical practice we have encountered situations in which other devices failed to provide relief. Second, we live in a country that witnessed the emergence of fraternal social bonds thanks to self-organization strategies developed in times of state violence and social crisis. The Mothers and Grandmothers of Plaza de Mayo, neighborhood assemblies, and soup kitchens are some relevant examples.

44 Couples and families today

The current theoretical and clinical literature on the sibling complex is broad and varied. Kancyper (2004) emphasizes the relevance of this complex for the development of both individual and social psychic life, and stresses its irreducible specificity and its interaction with narcissistic and Oedipal dynamics. According to this author, "the inclusion of fraternal psychodynamics does not undermine . . . the crucial role played by Narcissus and Oedipus in the shaping of psychic life" (2003, p. 139). The Oedipus and sibling complexes are different but interdependent factors at play in the creation of rules at the individual and the cultural levels (Moscona, 2003). The Freudian myth of the horde discussed in *Totem and Taboo* shows that brotherhood is based on the murder of the primal father.

In view of the increasing weakness of the social institutions that used to provide a support network, a new perspective on the fraternal bond has emerged that considers it an alternative path toward subjectivation. In Droeven's words, "siblinghood is organized not only in family practices but also in social discourses and practices. Siblings' histories, then, will be constitutively affected by historical processes" (Droeven, 2002, p. 19). It develops as a horizontal structure that brings peers together. Besides requiring participants to accept differences and the individual characteristics of each of its members, the fraternal relationship offers an alternative to narcissistic withdrawal as well as to the lack of identification models. The fraternal bond calls into question the aspiration to a single law.

New epistemological viewpoints have moved away from the conception of a rational Cartesian subject. Modern theoretical models and their fixed, preestablished, and closed relationships have been left behind. Assoun (2000, p. 15) expounds on the fraternal bond as an intermediate element between one's relationship with oneself and one's relationship with others, as a "bridge between Narcissus and Oedipus." Matus (2003) expands this idea. She argues that the fraternal link can transform by evolving from narcissistic specularity to social solidarity.

We believe that fraternal links are relevant in that they serve as a supplement to Oedipal relations. Supplementing is neither substituting nor complementing. According to Moreno, "complementing means using something that is allegedly missing to achieve a preconceived unity without altering this unity." Supplementing, instead, means adding in the same way as the newspaper supplements add to its main body. "Supplementation," states this author, "is what happens when a radically new emergent detotalizes a previously established conception" (Moreno, 2014, p. 116).

The possibility opened by fraternal links does not undermine or disturb the instituting quality of the Oedipus complex. "The supplement," claims Lewkowicz, "introduces complexity without integrating, becomes part of a network without blending, and modifies the other elements without antagonizing" (Lewkowicz, 2002, p. 296).

The stages of fraternal links

Gaspari (2003) describes three stages or periods of fraternal bonds that do not necessarily succeed one another and can even be simultaneous: suppression, conjunction, and differentiation. Our aim is to connect these stages with the different forms assumed by fraternal configurations described by Droeven and other authors. Among these configurations are parent-child, sibling-child, and sibling-sibling.

The first period, during which rivalry is suppressed, corresponds to the Cain and Abel story; it is "either I or the other." At this stage the relationship between siblings has no autonomy. We could say that it takes place around the parent-child link. Siblings vie for parents' love. The union-conjunction period, in turn, is associated with the establishment of siblinghood. This stage is characterized by the shift from rivalry to complicity, but the parental injunction continues to play a leading role. The relationship revolves around the fraternal-filial link.

Finally, the period described as differentiation-separation will pave the way for the establishment of the fraternal alliance. At this stage, the relationship revolves around the sibling-sibling link. This period inaugurates the idea of a new law that transcends the law of the father. At this point, self-organization processes prevail – immanent rules and processes that make alliances possible.

It is at this stage that social networks are conceived and built and acquire a variety of configurations that exceed family connections. They involve the opening to the exogamic exit and to forging bonds with peers. Asymmetry and parity are simultaneously established, and differences are signified in fraternal rather than parent-child terms. We witness the appearance of expressions of solidarity typical of friendship.

Self-organization is nurtured and shaped by interactions. While it does not exist outside them, it is relatively autonomous and stable. It is sustained by multiple ties and interrelating gestures that produce effects and meaning. The existence of an immanent, fraternal, and horizontal law that produces subjectivity and has the ability to transform is consistent with Foucault's (1978) concept of capillary power. In this author's view, what drives or thwarts society is countless small powers rather than the action of a central power. The idea of multiple powers that circulate through society as through capillaries and create a play of forces parts ways with the notion of a hegemonic power, for these small powers operate like a reticular organization.

The collapse of vertical power in postmodern times has driven subjects to take refuge in a horizontal network of peers. Friendship, for instance, inhabits a world with some constraints but more freedom. We emphasize the value of the meeting and of fraternal links, of which friendship, a

46 Couples and families today

chosen fraternal bond, is a sublimated offshoot (Kancyper, 2003). In Castro Orellana's words,

> friendship is not alien to power and resistance relations. It is practiced within a *strategic situation* and responds to the work of an *art of living* that seeks to minimize situations of domination . . . friendship is an ethics of the power play, a wisdom of distance and proximity vis-à-vis the other.
>
> (Castro Orellana, 2008, p. 491; his emphasis)

Horizontal bonds

Fraternal bonds have acquired new meanings in the current social context. Participating and getting involved in social life is also a way of playing a leading role as siblings. Not long ago we enjoyed a visit of the West-Eastern Divan Orchestra, created with talented and humanitarian commitment by Daniel Barenboim and Edward Said. Barenboim and Said devoted themselves to the challenge of building a fraternal experience of coexistence among Israeli, Palestinian, and other Arab musicians. Orchestra members must become part of the group by playing with and listening to each other, by being alike and different at the same time. This orchestra has crossed borders and blurred the rigid boundaries that undermine fraternal relations among nations.

In this way, being part of fraternal scenarios nurtures both individual identities and the social fabric. Friendship, hospitality, adherence to and membership in institutions, political and professional affiliations, as well as other peer configurations contribute to our life in common. These relationships, grounded in horizontality, create a space for the difficult exercise of tolerance.

Figures of identical twinship

Similar, different, identical; we are always comparing. The counterpoint between similarity and difference is amusing and alluring. This tension between homogeneity and heterogeneity has identical twinship as its paradigmatic figure. Freud (1919) gives us an example of the effect of this figure in his essay on "The Uncanny." There he relates an episode that occurred to him during a train trip. He was sitting in his compartment when the train stopped suddenly, causing the door of the adjoining bathroom to open, and "an elderly gentleman in a dressing-gown and a travelling cap came in."

Thinking that the elderly gentleman had taken a wrong turn in leaving the bathroom, Freud jumps up, ready to send him in the right direction. Yet that was not the case: "I at once realized to my dismay that the intruder was nothing but my own reflection in the looking-glass on the open door. I can still recollect that I thoroughly disliked his appearance" (Freud, 1919, p. 248). Nothing is more distressing than not being unique. The unexpected encounter with the identical grounds Freud's views on what he calls "the uncanny." He describes it as an experience of alienation that arouses fear or terror toward something that is actually familiar to us.

In the collective imagination, the identical seizes our attention. It arouses curiosity. It appeals and fascinates. The identical twin phenomenon skirts the boundary of castration by cherishing the fantasy that we are completed and perpetuated in that other who is just like us. Moreover, it awakens the illusion of immortality and transcendence.

There are many figures of identical twinship; some are biological, while others are virtual, imaginary, or social. There are pairs of identical twins that highlight similarities and reinforce indiscrimination by perpetuating the idea of a duplicate rather than the idea of *an other*. To avoid confusing them, those around them must find traits that are specific to each. Yet there isn't always a birthmark that might save us. Moreover, the mysterious imaginary friend may be considered a form of temporary twinship. That invisible tenant created by some children in their fantasy is generally made up to their own image and likeness.

Of course, creative displays of extreme resemblance have a true aesthetic impact. There are numerous examples of identical twinship in literature and the arts. During the 2012 Olympic Games in London, we enjoyed the water show offered by the Sánchez twins as a symmetrical synchronized swimming duet. Saramago (2005) starts the plot of his novel *The Double* with the shock suffered by a spectator who discovers a character on the movie screen who is identical to him. He gets so exasperated that he devotes himself to finding his double.

Still, even identical twins can establish fraternal relationships. When singularities are recognized and accepted, there is room for otherness, interdependence, and self-organization. Differences can hence emerge. When the fraternal constellation is trained in interdependence, we can speak of supplementary twinship.

The current social context has given new momentum to the question of twinship, both through new reproductive technologies that have increased the number of multiple pregnancies and through the use of the medical scalpel in plastic surgery. Furthermore, human cloning, confined, until recently, to the realm of fiction, would possibly be a new and powerful tool to create identical twins. This technology could causes filiation, consanguinity, and parenting bonds to collapse. Cloning, the paradigm of genetic manipulation, arouses deep concern and anxiety.

Salvador Dalí speaks openly in his autobiography about the pain of having been preceded by a dead brother also named Salvador. "I lived through my death before living my life," he claims. "At the age of seven

48 Couples and families today

my brother died of meningitis, three years before I was born. This shook my mother to the very depths of her being. . . . She was never to get over it" (Dalí, 1976, p. 12). And later he adds: "Born double, with an extra brother, I had to kill him off in order to assume my own place" (ibid., p. 47). In other words, there is no copy or replacement.

Van Gogh also suffered the presence of a dead brother, his double, who died a year before the painter's birth and was called Vincent like him. Every morning and evening during his school years, the future artist would walk past the cemetery and read his own name on a grave. We wonder to what extent this traumatic situation may have shaped the singular fraternal bond between Vincent and Theo.

There may also be a perverse use of an identical twin condition. Such was the case of Ivan and Sam, age 35, who both used cocaine in high doses. Each of them underwent individual analysis and link therapy. The unconscious pact that supported them aimed to maintain their uniqueness. By way of this mode of linking, they desperately sought to be completed by the other. Symbiotic lack of discrimination and omnipotent magical thinking predominated in both their thoughts and their actions. Through corrupt covenants, they sought to perpetuate and exploit the original state of fusion. We call this type of twinship *con-fusion*. These brothers resorted to encapsulated secrets and alliances as psychopathic strategies to manipulate the external world.

There are, in our view, other veiled, covert, and foreboding modes of identical twinship. Contemporary subjectivity is torn between a tendency to make us believe that we are unique and the homogeneity imposed by globalization. Replicas, spare clones, faithful copies do not replace the original. If uniformity prevails at the expense of diversity, the actual richness of nuances, contrasts, and differences is lost.

Chapter 6

On clinical interventions

The initial interview

Andrés, who is 40 years old, seeks consultation because he is having difficulties in his relationship with his daughters. Sandra is 13, and Ariela eight. He divorced his wife almost two years ago and has been in individual analysis for four years. He asks to be seen together with his daughters. He describes violent fights with his ex-wife that have persisted even after their separation and have impeded almost any form of communication between them. He does not know how to address this situation. Violence scares and repulses him. He chooses not to see his daughters in order to avoid conflict. Yet he wants to reflect on what is happening to him because he is afraid of losing his bond with them.

Andrés says that Sandra is quiet and that is hard for him to know what is going on with her. He has noticed that she is sad and that she is very much like him – she withdraws in order to escape conflict. Ariela, by contrast, is short-tempered, quarrelsome, and aggressive. "Just like her mother. Sometimes it's hard for me to realize that she's a different person and not the childhood version of my ex-wife." Ariela insults and yells at him, and sometimes threatens to hit him. She has a fit when she is contradicted; she throws herself on the ground, kicks out, and cries. Yet it was a fight between the sisters a week earlier that compelled him to ask for help.

"They insulted and hit each other; they pulled each other's hair. They ended up on the floor crying and kicking each other. They have always fought, they seem like enemies, and lately they've been worse. But if they're not together, they need to know what the other is doing. Generally, it's Ariela who starts the fight. She gets angry if Sandra doesn't answer her right away or refuses to lend her something or to do the favor she needs right now. Sandra ignores her; she won't answer, or will answer in monosyllables. What struck me about this fight is that it was so sudden, everything happened in a few seconds. I was in the bathroom, and when I came out it was chaos."

50 Couples and families today

The analyst decides to have the three of them come to the second interview. In link clinical practice an event may occur that will simultaneously change the logics of psychic functioning of all the members of that link. If participants are faithful to the link, new effects of meaning or the construction of participants' subjectivity will ensue.

The second interview

Ariela comes in carrying a soda can and a bag of potato chips. She says hello with food in her mouth. She is wearing her school smock[1] and carrying her backpack. The father says he spoke with his daughters about the need to start a therapy that would help them get along better. Ariela complains that she does not have enough time to do her homework. The father tries to explain to her that she will have enough time. Ariela gets angry and tells him to shut up, and claims that he is "talking bullshit." The father reprimands her because of her language. Ariela intensifies her verbal aggression.

The analyst intervenes. She introduces herself, makes a reference to the first interview with the father, and adds that she decided to gather the three of them so that they could ponder together what is going on and their difficulty in relating to each other. She asks Ariela and Sandra what they think about this idea. Ariela immediately answers that she wants to come, while Sandra says it doesn't make any difference to her: "If we have to come, I'll come." The father states that they cannot do it on their own, that they need help. The analyst tries to generate an atmosphere that will allow them to think about the causes of their discomfort.

Assessment interviews are indispensable both as a diagnostic tool and to inform the development of a suitable therapeutic device. They configure an initial space, "the prologue time," according to Aulagnier (1984).

The treatment of this family lasted about three years. In this chapter we will only point to some issues related to the analytic device and the fraternal link. During the first stretch of the treatment, sessions progressed in a difficult, tense atmosphere, amid Ariela's frequent violent outbursts, the father's anger and despair, and Sandra's silence. They had a hard time facing something that overwhelmed them. Erasers and other small objects would repeatedly fly across the room, hurled by one sister to the other.

Once, a very angry Ariela threw a pencil holder at Sandra's head, and Sandra retaliated with a shoe. The analyst stood up and said that they could not continue with the therapy if this behavior persisted. When situations characterized by excess or loss of control cannot be restrained by way of interpretations, other types of intervention are required that do not resort to metaphor to produce an effect. Such interventions also aim to reinstate the space of analysis. In these cases, interrupting the session constitutes a therapeutic strategy, an intervention by means of an act. It indicates that certain conditions are making it impossible to continue with the therapeutic work. It sets a boundary.

Up until then, the climate between the sisters had been of rivalry and confrontation. It seemed that they shared the conviction that there was not enough space for both of them. It was a time of suppression that was traversed by the logic of disjunction: either I or the other. When violence permeates the parental link, it may sometimes transform children in the *symptom-bearers* (Kaës, 2006) of the difficulties and conflicts that were not processed in the space of parents interaction. In this context, the siblings cannot establish a "fraternal alliance." When the family sought help, Ariela and Sandra were sisters in the biological sense – their being sisters was based on the act of filiation. Their link was founded on the parent-child relationship.

Early on in the treatment, the analyst stated openly and repeatedly that Sandra's silence was eloquent and a cause for concern, for Sandra did not know what she was expressing with it. Shortly after the start of the therapy Sandra was hospitalized with a bleeding ulcer. The lack of binding had led to a bodily outburst. The non-processed conflict was expressed in the body, outside the representational field.[2]

This episode created a sensitive situation. Distressed by Sandra's unexpected hospitalization, the girls' mother, whom the analyst had not met, demanded that the analyst terminate the therapy of the father and the daughters and start treating Sandra individually, and at another time asked to be included in the link sessions. Despite the pressure, the analyst decided to maintain the link space as the father and his two daughters had configured it. At first, she offered the mother to attend an individual interview that never took place. Some time later, the analyst referred the girl to a colleague with whom she started a psychoanalytic treatment.

While the analyst recognized the need for a multifaceted approach, she considered it advisable to develop the device as the analytic work unfolded. Sandra's referral to an individual analysis was part of the therapeutic device. Indications are decisions, and they entail an analytic act.

After her hospitalization, Sandra became more involved. The analyst sought to build bridges by offering "transition symbol formations" (Bleichmar, 2005) that would promote the patients' coming into contact with those elements that lay outside the chain of signifiers. The idea was to achieve the highest degree of symbolization by intruding as little as possible. Representations suggested by the analyst may succeed in organizing excitations (Raitzin de Vidal, 2010). Through these first bindings, some of the violence and helplessness is contained and becomes part of the web.

> Sandra started talking, and different sources of discomfort emerged in her words: her isolation, her difficulty in making friends, and her being tired of fights, which were the major mode of exchange in the

relationship. Her bleeding ulcer and subsequent hospitalization were the evidence of a suffering that she could only now start to verbalize. While her participation was still limited, it allowed us to glimpse the effects that the circulating violence was having on her. At the same time, by breaking her hermetic silence, she helped relieve the tense atmosphere.

Another shift occurred when Ariela started first to draw and later to "take notes." This development makes us think about the role of individual productions in link therapy. Ariela's drawings and notes traced working-through paths for the entire family. For the analyst, in turn, they constituted a kind of document, evidence of the road traveled so far that enabled her to assess the evolution of the treatment.

We were struck by the fact that Ariela chose graphic series. Work in series implies the creation of a set of interconnected drawings. In each of them there are similar elements that facilitate their identification as part of a group, and different elements that indicate that each drawing constitutes a unique production. In this interplay of similarities and differences something new starts to materialize. " 'The real is grasped in pieces,' says Vainstoc, quoting Lacan, and adds, *'in pieces of series developed a posteriori'* " (Vainstoc, 2003, p. 432; author's emphasis).

From the series of the pairs to the series of writings

These were the first drawings made by Ariela during the family hour (see Figures 6.1 and 6.2). Ariela said they were separate things. We observed, however, that there were several objects organized as symmetrical or complementary pairs, like a hammer and a nail, set up as though mirroring each other and spread through the page. The objects are simple, and the pairs are dynamic; they suffer transformations. In the first drawing some of the objects show closed designs, while in later productions the same series opens up. At the same time, drawings that were initially whole are incomplete in later versions.

Object series – symmetrical pairs

While the drawings are Ariela's production, they facilitate the mise en scène of the family drama, which unfolds in the course of the sessions. The pairs transform as the link work progresses. A process begins whereby family members seek to grasp differences in their psychic constitution, an insight that will allow them to avoid the specular functioning in which they are now immersed. Differences and ties grow simultaneously. As Gomel and Matus state, "We must distinguish between being siblings in

Figure 6.1 Ariela drawing 1

Figure 6.2 Ariela drawing 2

54 Couples and families today

the sense of being named as such by the parents, and coming together as siblings (*hermanarse*). The latter is the process of creation and maintenance of linking among siblings" (Gomel and Matus, p. 58).

Hands series

Ariela starts tracing her hands (see Figure 6.3). Across history, drawing one's hand has been a characteristic way of materializing an identity, of leaving a mark. The same hands that throw objects, hit, shove, and pull hair are now drawing themselves. Is this an attempt to restrain impulses? A way of starting to draw boundaries?

All the hands are adorned with long nails painted red and with rings, and have watches. We should recall here Ariela's comment in the first family interview regarding her concern with time. We believe that the insistence in marking the passage of time also alludes to the parents' divorce; by introducing a break, a lack of continuity, difference is introduced. When the parents live together, an imaginary of "forever" tends to be created that involves a seamless continuity.[3]

While decorated hands bring to the fore Ariela's inquiry into femininity and her masturbatory aspects, it is worth looking at this material from a link perspective. In one of the drawings, along with a heart and a telephone communication network, she wrote, "hello, hello, hello," and beside these words, another text that reads, "someone is looking the other way." Could the fights between the sisters be a manner of saying, "Hello . . . I'm calling" so that someone would pay attention and not look the other way? Do they want to believe, imaginarily, that they will thus be able to stop the constant fights between the parents? Or could it be a way of showing the lack of family communication, in the fashion of a broken telephone?

Set series

The sets build configurations of flowers, birds, butterflies, stars, and so on. They resemble families of objects. Each set is enclosed by a figure, in the manner of a frame, forming complex designs. While sets are contained within wraps that bear different forms, there are always connections among the objects in each set.[4] At this time Ariela no longer draws pairs; she draws framed sets (see Figure 6.4). We can also relate these drawings to a shift in the family dynamics. A different organization starts to emerge that has borders.

For the fraternal link, this is a time of conjunction. There is now a space that has room for both sisters, and they can meet. The relationship still hinges on the fraternal-filial connection, but the process of coming together has already started. Their choosing each other as sisters alludes to an instituting operation. Gradually adopting each other as sisters involves

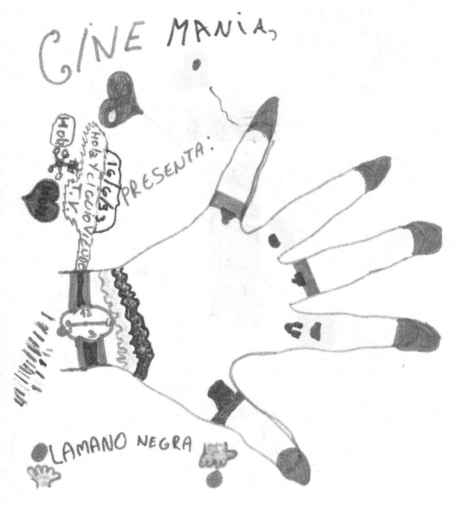

Figure 6.3 Ariela's hand drawing

Figure 6.4 Ariela's ensembles drawings

On clinical interventions 57

becoming close (*hermanarse*) in response to a desire. *Gradually* suggests a non-linear process that is subject to oscillations (Gomel and Matus, 2011).

Writing series

The three earlier series were produced along with another one that revealed a different quality. We have called it the writing series. The drawing and the writing were happening simultaneously rather than successively, for Ariela drew and wrote since the beginning of the treatment. She started by taking thorough notes of everything everyone said, in a manner of minutes. At first it seemed as though she were transcribing the sessions. She used different colors for each participant, and wrote the name of the speaker in parentheses. Her efforts to mark differences were remarkable. She inaugurated her writing with an eloquent phrase: "It's hard to contain Ariela (Dad)." In the same page there are some confusing phrases and a clear, descriptive one that reads, "Sandra coughs. Dad sighs. Silvia talks. I write."

This is a curious description; the father and Sandra are identified by a bodily action, while Ariela and the analyst have words in common. In later writings, Ariela no longer needs to distinguish the discourse of each participant with a color code. Discourse itself has acquired enough prominence. In our view, this is a "joint free narrative"[5] akin to free association in individual treatments. Ariela is a sensitive chronicler of things that move, distress, or concern family members. The effects of meaning are generated in a space beyond the individual psyche.

Ariela's writings gradually expand the dimension of inquiry, and the questions that worry them start to emerge. Yet not everybody will work through the shared meaning in the same way; this meaning will uniquely articulate in each participant. There is a constant back and forth between individual phrases and the family discourse.

Similarly, differences are slowly materialized through Ariela's drawings and writings, and aggressiveness and ambivalence are progressively processed and transformed. To illustrate this process, we have transcribed some of the phrases written during the sessions:

When you approach her, you see that she's quiet. You can't really expect what's gnawing at her to change.
It wasn't easy for me!
What does it mean to feel like it?
There aren't two sides here, there's only one side.
He tries not to see the mother in them.
The girls need to be given permission.
This is a job. I'm starting to realize.
They would never see each other again if they didn't share two daughters. It's hard to live like this. When they have to fulfill their role as parents.

58 Couples and families today

My ex-wife!!!!
The bottom line here is . . .
Everything that needs to be done for their sake, I do. I support them.
*According to my dad there are different payments, but in our minds, it's that Dad
and Mom are fighting. Mom brings one thing and Dad brings another. There's
stagnation.*
It's very hard to . . .
Am I being clear? More or less?
Sometimes there's no need to call each other names. We have to talk, to express.
There's more calm.
I'm sleepy.
My sister corrects me.
I ask a lot of questions so that things become clear to me.
So that things become clear to us in everyday life and in the world of feelings.
The problem between Mom and Dad sometimes causes routine (everyday) problems.

Odd words; faltering, highlighted, and underlined phrases. In reading
them, meanings emerge that portray the unfolding link interaction. Ariela
has stopped yelling. Now she transcribes what takes place in the sessions.
By way of her writing, she seeks to contain excess and create some kind of
symbolic anchorage, some binding – to leave a mark. Perhaps words acquire
a different consistency and may find a playful destiny. At the end of each
session the analyst asks Ariela if she wants to read what she wrote, and Ariela does. Step by step, the written phrases trace an itinerary: violence, the
need to prevail, confusion, the search for spaces for thinking and difference.
   Ariela writes:

   "There is anger. Fights. I want this; I want that."
   "To be able to think: this, yes; this, no. Each person is different."

Confusion also surrounds the parents' separation.
"Are we visiting or not?" Ariela writes.

   "Can we call it a different way? I'm going home. My home is your
   home. My home is where I live."

These phrases gradually form a question: "Which one is home?" Do
they have two homes? To whom does each home belong?
   Ariela also writes about jealousy.
   "Jealousy. How did we get to my being jealous?"
   At certain times, indiscriminate (fusion) aspects and visible and invisible
violence became relevant. The father generated violence in Ariela when he
attached a negative meaning to her expressions. He could perceive the
active violence that characterized Ariela and his ex-wife's behavior, but

ignored the violence by omission exercised by Sandra and sometimes by him. At other times there were associations with mourning.

Following Morin (2008), we consider that the link is a multifaceted, complex, and paradoxical organization that develops along with the subjects who establish the connection. Links are affected by the discursive, representational, and meaningful dimension, which organizes a way of functioning and interacting with others. The link constructs subjects who, in turn, construct the link in a process of becoming traversed by temporality. Link theory and its clinical practice face us with the multiple, the "in-between." The link connotes a different psychic reality.

As the treatment progresses, father and daughters can review their previous history and compose a new relationship. In this way, new linking spaces are designed. The relationship between the sisters starts to become clearer and to reveal its own dynamics – jealousy and rivalry, but also play and camaraderie. The increasing complexity of the linking space allows us to distinguish the different bindings that coexist simultaneously and successively. One of these bindings is transcendental in that it corresponds to a vertical authority, that is, is tied to the parental injunction and founded on the parent-child relationship; the other, an immanent mode of operation, is a product of the sibling group's self-organization.

Fraternity is another instance of symbolization of alterity, another possible mode of subjective production where parity facilitates the encounter with the fellow being and the construction of solidarity feelings. The idea that siblings may come together more freely, with a certain independence from the family imaginary, produces unprecedented effects that set in motion alternative logics. In this way, the field is open to other subjectivity productions (Droeven, 2002).

Specifications concerning our psychoanalytic practice

The heterogeneity of the resources used in link analysis significantly enlarges the scope of analyzable cases and opens new fields for psychoanalysis. Our willingness to make room for and legitimate these fields in their different variants is unavoidable. In each case, our clinical practice involves designing a device and setting it in motion. The type of device we choose is already a form of intervention. We understand intervention as "entering the game," "coming between."[6] Analysts "come between" in a field where transference, countertransference, and interference phenomena are also at play.

There are interventions that have an immobilizing effect and thus emphasize the path of repetition. Others have no effect at all, either because the timing was wrong or because the language used was not suitable. There are also interventions that allow creative play, that do not cancel

60 Couples and families today

difference. These cause surprise because they reveal the foreignness/alterity of the other.

Interpretations, observations, interventions by way of acts intended to preserve the work space and check patients' impulsiveness. Lack of control and violence are some possible modes of intervention. Constructions, observations, contextualizations that sustain a vacillating narcissistic web, questions aimed to break ties whose meaning has been naturalized and connect seemingly disjointed phrases, and the use of humor to emphasize or highlight a signifier, a repetition, a compelling phrase are also forms of intervention.

In child psychoanalysis, we tend to favor playful interpretations, as Rodrigué (1966) calls them. Analysts who play can intervene by dramatically interpreting from within the game without interrupting its progress. If they emerge from the depths of the patient-analyst play, playful interpretations will not be experienced as foreign. Children will have a greater chance of returning to them through the characters they create and process them through play.

Analysts' interventions may operate as a break that facilitates the creation of a signifier chain. In view of the drive overflow produced by this family in the sessions, interventions contributed to curbing this excess as well as the drive release expressed both through acting-out episodes and physical outbursts. Andrés and his daughters agreed to take part in joint sessions with varying levels of personal engagement at different times. Andrés maintained the link device with his presence and active participation, and was able to cope with the feelings of helplessness and hopelessness that overpowered him every now and then. As a result of link work, the analyst made the decision to preserve the link space as it had been envisioned from the start, that is, without the mother. Acknowledging the parents' separation opened the way for mourning.

The link device constitutes a suitable space for the dramatic unfolding of a story that is expressed in patients' ways of listening, talking, and looking at others (sexual, verbal, economic, emotional, or ideological exchanges). The choice between link and individual devices will depend on the identification of the right indication for that stage of the process and will respond to the specificities of each stage. Still, these devices do not oppose each other, nor do they rely on different theoretical frameworks.

Developing psychoanalytic devices means expanding the options provided by traditional clinical intervention. Link analysis offers participants an opportunity to see themselves as subjects who are sharing a situation with other subjects. This transference interplay operates against the grain of the weakening of ties, a weakening that is typical of family and social milieus that promote the emergence of fragmented links. As the link treatment unfolds, collective creation defines a field where singularities can multiply thanks to participants' unique appropriation of their conflicts and symptoms and their ability to do something with them.

The gaze and the scene, which includes everyone, generate a transference and countertransference space where multiple and reciprocal implications interact. In this particular case, addressing the situation by way of a family device was effective because it fostered the ability to produce a new arrangement and a different libidinal distribution. Belonging in a link involves a "work effort" on the part of each subject of the link. All link participants must work toward setting boundaries to individual identity and opening up to linking, to the dimension of the foreign in themselves and in others. *What takes place in the link is new and goes beyond each participant's productions* (Berenstein, 2004b).

As the representational field became more complex, the family group was able to find different forms of drive satisfaction and expand the sphere of link responsibility. A creative environment developed over the course of the sessions that reduced the violence that tends to erupt in non-differentiated spaces and facilitated work on symbol formation and differentiation.

Notes

1 In Argentine public schools students must wear a white smock over their clothes.
2 We consider that the concept of *essential depression* coined by P. Marty (2010) is very useful to understand Sandra's problems. This concept refers to the reaction to traumatic events that overwhelm patients' working-through capacity, a condition that suggests the disorganization of certain psychic functions. Desires vanish, and interests become machine-like. Representations are poor, and there is an absence of personal ideas. Facts and gestures lack imaginary value. This condition may expand and produce an explosion at the somatic level.
3 The authors use the term *hiancia*, the translation into Spanish of Lacan's term *béance*, which has been rendered into English in a variety of ways, among them, gap, gaping hole, and abyss.
4 Particularly in the case of children, the drawing as a fixed image could be a tool to harness anxiety-provoking experiences where images succeed one another in their minds with dizzying speed, appearing as inaccessible (Levin, 2003).
5 The concept of *joint free narrative* has been extensively discussed by various authors within the Asociación Argentina de Psicología y Psicoterapia de de Grupos (Argentine Association of Group Psychology and Psychotherapy).
6 The word in Spanish for "to intervene" is "intervenir," and "venir" means "to come." Thence "venir entre," or "come between."

Chapter 7

The fraternal dimension and trauma

Introduction

It is in relation to a fellow human-being that a human-being learns to cognize.
Sigmund Freud[1]

As primordial others, fellow beings play a role in psychic life that is both foundational and traumatic. In this sense, foundation and trauma are equivalent. We are referring here to trauma not as the cause of neurosis but in a broader sense, as constituting the psychic apparatus.

We consider fraternal wefts as primary links, and are particularly interested in examining the vicissitudes of these wefts throughout the processing of trauma. Our interest is both theoretical and clinical. We aim to look into their meaning and effect in our work. To this end, we discuss clinical vignettes from the analysis of two groups of siblings at the beginning of their treatment.

From the fellow-being complex to the fraternal partnership

To explore fraternal wefts, we start with a theoretical concept developed in the early days of psychoanalysis, namely, the fellow-being complex. Our itinerary will take us from this concept to the notion of fraternal partnership. Freud already talks about the *Nebenmensch* (fellow being) in the *Project for a Scientific Psychology* (Freud, 1895). This concept points to the foundational role of the fellow being in the development of both the psychic apparatus and thought. It is discordance rather than agreement that provides the impetus for the work of thought. When the object lends itself to perception, it becomes a fellow being. For the subject, the fellow being is at the same time the "first satisfying object and further his first hostile object, as well as his sole helping power. For this reason it is in relation to a fellow-human-being that a human-being learns to cognize" (Freud, 1895, p. 331).

The fraternal dimension and trauma 63

Children develop into subjects thanks to relational networks. In this context, the encounter with the other is unavoidable and is marked by helplessness. Human helplessness grants the other a key place and role. According to Diana Rabinovich, "representation is inscribed on the backdrop of helplessness and the Other" (Rabinovich, 1990, p. 14). Laplanche (1989), in turn, states that *Hilflosigkeit* is a helpless state in which, having been left to its own devices, the being cannot help itself. Consequently, it needs the help of another, or *fremde Hilfe* in Freud's terms.

The fellow-being complex bears two components. One "corresponds to a constant assemblage" (*das Ding*), the Thing, which presents itself as foreign and irreducible and alludes to the irretrievable dimension of the object. The other is the quality, the attribute that can be understood by memory as long as it refers to "the body and the experience of the subject" (Rabinovich, 1990, p. 16). From the *Nebenmensch* experience emerges *Fremde*, the foreign, the different, a stunning formula according to Lacan. In this author's words, "it expresses powerfully the idea of beside yet alike, separation and identity" (Lacan, 1992, p. 51). Thus, the fellow being is both close and *Fremde*, alien. "The whole progress of the subject is then oriented around the *Ding* as *Fremde*, . . . the first outside" (ibid., p. 52).

The *Nebenmensch* complex introduces the idea of alienness as different from alterity. Alienness cannot be thought or represented; alterity, by contrast, can be recognized. The alien is impossible to assimilate – it lacks representation and is hence irreducible. In Lacanian terms, similarity, alterity, and foreignness could correspond to the imaginary, symbolical, and real elements that structure every link. These three registers are always present and always interconnected. The *Nebenmensch* complex would serve as a mold for partnerships.

Later Freud refers to the "band of brothers" as the first form of social organization, which comprises a "renunciation of instinctual gratification; [a] recognition of mutual obligations; [and] institutions declared sacred, which could not be broken" (Freud, 1939, p. 104). It represents the shift from the fraternal bond to the partnership. After the murder of the father, the brothers "formed the totemic community of brothers, all with equal rights and united by the totem prohibitions" (Freud, 1922, p. 134). This is how morality and the law were born. After the murder of the father, when the totemic brotherhood is constituted, its members realize that they are brothers.

We could say that identification lies at the core of the fraternal partnership. As Freud formulates it, identification is the first mode of affective connection with another person. It "result[s] among other things in a person limiting his aggressiveness towards those with whom he has identified himself, and in his sparing them and giving them help" (Freud, ibid., p. 53).

At the same time, ambivalent from the start, identification precedes the investiture of the object. The shift from the fraternal bond to a partnership

64   Couples and families today

will require, therefore, identification and, simultaneously, a differentiation process. The fraternal as a horizontal tie among peers brings into play the problem of sameness, associated with identification, and difference, tied to the acknowledgment of incompleteness and alienness. The fraternal unfolds as a tension between similarity and difference/alienness.

On the notion of trauma

The concept of trauma is present in most of Freud's writings, from the "Preliminary Communication" (1893, Breuer-Freud) to *Moses and Monotheism* (1939 [1934–1938]) and *An Outline of Psycho-Analysis* (1940 [1938]). However, it suffers transformations along this journey. Furthermore, it had already been significantly developed before the emergence of psychoanalysis. In pre-classic Greek culture, in the seventh century BC, trauma was associated with an experience that cannot be assimilated and places subjects at its mercy. By way of the Gorgon, a monstrosity combining human and beast that was both terrifying and grotesque, the Greek sought to represent the nonviable. As a result, trauma is tied to an inconsistency, namely, the search for a representation of the unrepresentable.

Trauma as effraction always refers to the idea of a stunned subject. It represents a disruption of everyday life – a loss of the illusion of continuity that faces us with the limits of the sayable. It is an experience that appears unexpectedly and eludes representation. The sudden, the unforeseen introduces the mark of temporality. Something that was experienced but is actually impossible to assimilate bursts into the life of an unprepared subject.

Assoun (2004) considers that the "height of trauma" is the subject's brutal encounter with a de-symbolizing situation, an implosion that, since it does not provoke a tear, a simultaneous wound, contributes to the disentangling of the drives. "The first time of the trauma remains mute until the *nachträglich* allows it to speak and to become trauma. The mute 'pre-traumatic' time of the trauma is as unassimilable, unrepresentable, unnamable as is the death instinct itself." (Baranger, Baranger, and Mom, 1988, p. 127).

We are dealing here with a temporality in two movements – with the delayed effect (*Nachträglichkeit*) of something that becomes effective in a second stage. The notions of mechanic causality and linear temporality thus lose validity. The trauma is structured in the modality of the *après-coup* and alters the dynamic balance of the drives. "The psychoneuroses are traumas with history" (ibid., p. 125). This is how Mom and W. and M. Baranger define neuroses in order to distinguish them from traumas that are not easily historicizable. We are referring to those aspects of pure trauma that may remain present yet are impossible to assimilate; like an impenetrable wall, they resist historicization.

There is no absolute traumatic event. Already in 1897, when Freud famously stated in a letter to Fliess, "I no longer believe in my *neurotica*" (September 21, 1897, in Masson, 1985, p. 264), fantasy life acquired great relevance. The abandonment of the theory of seduction renders the notion of trauma more complex by emphasizing its relative nature. Subjects respond with their uniqueness, depending on the ways in which the event resonates with their individual history and the position they adopt in the face of this experience.[2]

Since *Inhibitions, Symptom and Anxiety* (1926), the traumatic situation has referred to the state of helplessness (*Hilflozichkeit*). The difference between internal and external trauma disappears. Whatever its origin, trauma results in a flooding of the ego that reactivates its primordial state of powerlessness. "The brilliant thing about this theory," states Laplanche,

> is, of course, that it makes nonsense of later attempts to strike a balance between what is exogenous and what is endogenous, but at the same time everything is endogenous; the efficacy of the process stems from the moment of the endogenous reactivation of a memory which obviously derives from a real external event.
>
> (Laplanche, 1987, p. 113)

The stunned subject, submerged in perplexity, could also be stimulated to find new meanings. From this perspective, despite its paralyzing effect, trauma could give subjects the opportunity to create something new.

Even though Freud abandons the theory of seduction very early on, he does not "renounce the 'real' basis of the traumatic sexual situations, now seen in the form of universal and paradigmatic situations" (Baranger, Baranger, and Mom, 1988, p. 115). In this way, trauma loses its contingent value and becomes a foundational aspect of subjectivity; the drive is inscribed in a traumatic way. Aulagnier talks about a structuring primary violence, a libidinal offer that is also an offer of meaning and is marked by a foundational asymmetry.

In Laplanche's terms, signifiers coming from the adult, tied to the satisfaction of the helpless child's needs, carry enigmatic messages of a sexual nature that are hard to symbolize. The *theory of generalized seduction* alludes to the constitution of the psychic apparatus through a series of traumas. This author points to the presence of the parents' unconscious – of the adult, who faces the object-source that distresses him (Laplanche, 1989).

These authors' differing theoretical approaches contain a similar idea, which we share. Trauma is a foundational aspect of the psychic apparatus, and primordial links are both structuring and traumatic.

The "band of brothers": a possible way of weaving a weft with helplessness

Based on these initial, perhaps mythical, stages, we became interested in inquiring into the potential destinies offered by fraternity, in the sense of *band of brothers*, as a means of processing trauma. Such processing will hinge on the binding and unbinding that subjects are able to perform in order to skirt, veil, and weave the unnamable real into the representational weft in the face of a situation of helplessness. Clinical practice provides manifold variations depending on singular vicissitudes and the unfolding of the tension between sameness and difference, homogeneity and heterogeneity. In what follows we describe some of these variations.

Gina and Mora, four-year-old twins, arrive together for a diagnostic interview. The father is concerned because his ex-wife, the mother of the girls, has been hospitalized for seven months after repeated suicide attempts. He is seeking guidance concerning his daughters. The girls live with him and his mother. His ex-wife will not be discharged any time soon, and her prognosis is uncertain. We have included this vignette for two reasons. First, it corresponds to a request for a psychoanalytic diagnosis regarding an allegedly traumatic situation. Second, the material allows us to articulate traumatic effects and the fraternal bond.

Gina and Mora, two very vital, self-confident girls, started the interview showing a willingness to explore, play, draw, and talk about themselves (which is curious, given their young age), their environment, and their family. Their behavior evinced no significant impediments, and their productions showed a level of psychic organization that was promising for their age (Figure 7.1, Figure 7.2).

Their activities did not overlap; Gina chose to draw, while Mora preferred to play. They naturally and willingly shared the various areas of the office and the available objects. They collaborated, openly criticized one another, and complemented each other's narratives. This way of organizing – resorting to joint self-regulation as a mode of satisfaction – may have protected them from further de-structuring. Trained to be mutually dependent, they conveyed an attitude of greater autonomy from adult support in the face of hardship.

The fraternal constellation may have softened the traumatic effects of living with a mother who was desperately seeking death. The analyst acted as a third; they only appealed to her for specific interventions when they encountered obstacles to their handling of play materials or to ask

Figure 7.1 Family

Figure 7.2 Sisters

questions that would satisfy their curiosity. The ease with which they separated from their father when they entered the office was also striking. Fraternal complicity had become a mode of survival. They provided each other with a guiding light, a shelter from the fragility of family support in this traumatic circumstance.

We could argue that this way of handling the mother's absence is predominantly based on the construction of an active, functional communicating connection between the sisters that partly mitigates the violent impact of the mother's disappearance from their everyday life. In sum, it is our hypothesis that the incidence of traumatic effects is reduced when a fraternal partnership serves as a shield from destruction and from the irruption in the psyche of excessive stimuli. This protective dimension becomes a potential resource to process situations of emotional exposure.

Identical twin brothers: the source of a traumatic psychic structuring?

This clinical narrative is about the beginning of a treatment of an 18-year-old young man. The choice of verbal and graphic material responds to a

68 Couples and families today

specific concern, namely, pondering the connection between his being an identical twin and his subjective development.

Joaquín was forced by his family to see a therapist. He agreed to come to an interview after spending forty-six days locked up in his room. Alarmed and concerned, his parents sought help due to the disruption to family life created by Joaquín's behavior. To agree to be helped, Joaquín demanded that his twin brother Juan be present at the interview. For the twins, their togetherness was both the way they came into the world and the way they came to the consulting room. Their closeness was a constant, essential presence throughout the treatment.

Joaquín would sporadically have an outburst in front of the mirror. He would tear away his face,[3] squeeze it, hurt it, mark it. Trapped in his imbalance, he struggled against an irresistible compulsion, a scourge that led to self-destruction. After these explosions he would shut himself away in his room and withdraw from everyone while he waited for his wounds to heal. Sometimes several weeks would go by before his skin would recover its homogeneous color and texture.

Something in the mirror eluded him. Was it his face? His twin brother's? Whom was he seeing? He would lose control and remain alienated, like a hostage who could not move freely. His mirror image seemed to belong to the other. Faced with this evidence, he was terrified. He injured and traumatized himself. "If it wasn't because of the face it wouldn't be an issue. I like to lift weights, be ripped. I'm an optician and I'm taking more courses to specialize in contact lenses," said Joaquín.

The signs of a traumatic incongruence in Joaquín's subjective development appeared almost at the beginning of the transference: "I was married to my brother for seventeen years; I never needed friends, he's my family." Joaquín's problems did not start when he separated from his brother. We are not dealing with a traumatic detachment but with a deficiency in his psychic structuring that was concealed by the fraternal relationship.

Agreeing with Levinas that "the human I is posited in fraternity" (Levinas, 1969, p. 279) means recognizing a significant articulation between the emergence and development of the ego, on the one hand, and the fraternal relationship, on the other. If this is the case, finding early deficiencies in both the constitution of the ego and the link between siblings may lead us to postulate a traumatic subjective structuring. Joaquín's complaint reveals the moment when he transforms past trauma into symptoms.

Joaquín insists that because he is identical to his brother, everybody searches his face to identify him; they look at him in order to retain some trace that suggests a difference. Joaquín feels that his face is the target (*blanco*) of everybody's shots, even his own. The face is blank (*en blanco*); there is no face. There is an outburst that hurts. There is resignation, pain, anxiety.

The fraternal dimension and trauma 69

Among the motifs that produce an uncanny effect, Freud includes the idea "of a 'double'" in every shape and degree, with persons, therefore, who are to be considered identical by reason of looking alike . . . so that his self becomes confounded, or the foreign self is substituted for his own.

(Freud, 1919, p. 234)

When Joaquín comes back into contact with the external world, which Juan represents, he is surprised, irritated. He feels he has been deprived of what he believes was his. He is hence left without a face that will identify him (see Figure 7.3). He cannot tolerate this misery; he becomes horrified and flees, traumatized.

Joaquín cannot become a subject. If the brothers are identical, does it mean one of them "is not"? Might this be the uncanny core of what distresses him? Does he feel he is going mad due to the rending caused by the sight of his split face? By disfiguring his face, he stages his tragedy. He

Figure 7.3 No face

70 Couples and families today

struggles with the narcissistic split suggested either by an identical fellow being who cannot, then, be another, or by an image of himself he cannot appropriate. It is a crossroads inscribed in the body that becomes uncanny, traumatic because it cannot be semanticized.

What Joaquín finds impossible to assimilate insists by way of compulsive repetition, with explosions that periodically destabilize him. We could think, therefore, that in this case being an identical twin had traumatic effects; it hindered the psychic structuring process. The violence of the duplicated and split image turned it into a terrifying figure, "just as after the fall of their religion," according to Freud, "the gods took on daemonic shapes" (Freud, 1919, p. 236). Levinas suggests an interesting relationship between face and violence. The face is exposed, threatened, as though inviting us to perform an act of violence. Yet, at the same time, it forbids us to kill. The coexisting temptation and inability to kill are inscribed in the face.

Joaquín's graphic productions in session evince a powerful but failed sadism. Such sadism is expressed in his drawing of the dinosaur (see Figure 7.4), whose hands are full of claws but short, almost like stumps (nails-fangs), and with which he could not touch his body, unfit for jouissance.

Figure 7.4 Violence

Many fangs, only fangs; we are dealing with a drawing that has been amputated from its ability to attack, a caricature of the violence embodied in the dinosaur.

Joaquín insists that he and his brother are two sides of the same coin: "With Juan I never needed anything." Can the two sides of the same coin meet? Could they recognize each other? It would seem that it is thanks to the mirror image that one can see the other side – of the same coin? According to W. Baranger (1991), this specular double constitutes the origin of the fraternal complex. Joaquín makes great efforts to prevent his brother from being the reflection that arouses him. If the one in the mirror is his brother, he himself is trapped in a homosexual jouissance that both satisfies and terrifies him.

The specular encounter brings about a tension between the identical and the foreign. The latter constitutes a core of subjectivity that cannot be reduced to the ego and that Freud includes in his description of the development of the fellow-being complex. Still, the mirror also deceives. As Rosset (2012) states so well, the mirror is the last opportunity to apprehend ourselves and will always disappoint us. The ego's search, especially in patients with splitting problems, is always tied to a kind of stubborn return to the mirror and to everything that may present an analogy with it. For instance, these patients show an obsession with symmetry in all its guises. Symmetry (see Figure 7.5) is akin to the mirror image; it does not offer the thing but its other, its reverse, its flip side, its projection.

The face harasses Joaquín and focuses his attention. In this way, he also attracts the others' gaze in his fantasy because, while he acknowledges no exteriority to the mirror image, neither can he appropriate it. This is when he becomes desperate and attacks his face. Soler (1988) explains this phenomenon with great lucidity and clarity when she discusses the case of Van Gogh. Shortly after painting a stunning work of art, the painter cuts his body, his image, which losses its symmetry. He needs to realize what he cannot symbolize by way of an act performed on his body – cutting his ear.

Joaquín seems to perforate his face. In his fantasy, only then will he be recognized in difference and sameness. We may view these marks that traumatize him as the lure that grants meaning to a deeper denunciation, that of an impossibility that is present in the very constitution of his subjectivity. In other words, being an identical twin involved a dual traversing of the traumatic; it was both the cause of the trauma and its concealment.

Configurations of the fraternal in social ties

> *The existence of the Other . . . concern[s] us in the collectivity.*
> Emmanuel Levinas[4]

Where did our particular interest in the fraternal link originate? We belong to societies where the paternal figure has faded. The fraternal dimension,

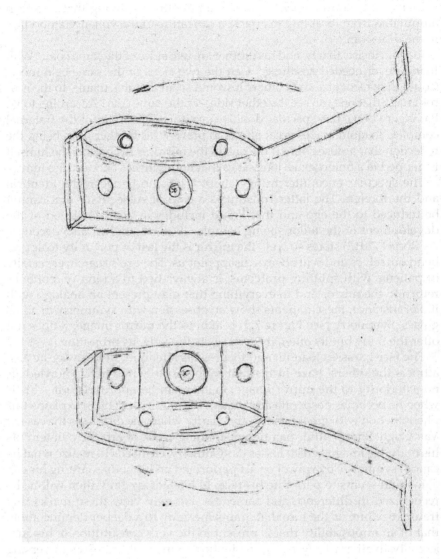

Figure 7.5 Symmetry

in turn, has emerged as an alternative to build social ties. Next we analyze the intertwining of subject, link, and culture. Our aim is to look at the fluctuations between brotherhood and fraternal partnership and understand how they operate in the social field.

Western culture is marked by a double threat. On the one hand, there is an increasing tendency toward homogeneity. On the other hand, paradoxically, there is a fragmenting tendency that segregates and expels. The mirror is broken; subjectivity cannot look at itself. In this context, we consider the existence of other ways of processing the transfigurations suffered by contemporary subjectivity.

Anxiety caused by helplessness exacerbates our inevitable need for a fellow being, an other who will mark our uniqueness through his or her diversity, alterity, alienness. The fragility of the infant, its lack of resources, and its motor and psychic helplessness defined the features of its support and care. Changes occurring in the last century left the adult world in a state of exposure, of powerlessness that undermined its resources (Kuras de Mauer and May, 2001). It is important to keep these developments in mind because the world of childhood and adolescence still needs an adult position that will protect it.

Unemployment, exclusion, depression, "dis-existence" are some of the traces of adversity that expose human beings to helplessness. These psychosocial disorders have configured a new set of problems that affect psychoanalytic practice. Psychoanalysts must hence seek new ways of thinking and of providing care that integrate the horizontal dimension. During the crisis suffered by Argentina in 2001, new modes of relationship emerged in a period marked by the weakness of the state and the impoverishment of its residents. Bartering among peers, horizontal swaps, and neighborhood assemblies gained relevance as primary exchange mechanisms. These forms of social mobilization and protest aspired to develop other modes of representation and new ideas. In its own way, each advanced an alternative legality.

Fraternal wefts contribute a wealth of vitality and movement in an attempt to exorcize and mitigate the devouring, nothingizing, and inertia effects of Thanatos in today's globalized world. These wefts lead to unprecedented, situational rituals that bring people together to cope with the pain of traumatic impact.[5] These rituals become symbolic references and favor the possibility of historicizing excess. They help veil and mitigate, to some extent, the defenselessness caused by the disproportionate real. In these practices the inevitable, close presence of the fellow being finds justification. An ethics of difference thereby emerges that favors joint doing and responsibility as major values.

As "bands of brothers," fraternal groups provide hitherto unprecedented link horizons that are built in a horizontal and immanent way. While sometimes ephemeral, they may eventually become the matrix for potential change and thus protect subjects from the irruption of trauma.

Fraternity as responsibility:
a psychoanalytic approach

We view responsibility as an articulating concept that helps us reflect on fraternal wefts. We aim to discuss its significance in psychoanalytic

74 Couples and families today

practice without neglecting the social field. While responsibility always refers to ethics, we are not talking about it in a judgmental or moral sense. According to Puget, being responsible entails making the decision to take responsibility for what happens in a certain situation. Such a decision does not precede the situation and always exceeds it (Puget, 2004).

As far as we are concerned, we believe that being responsible analysts involves the ability to adopt a responsible perspective and to let it guide our actions. In other words, we are not dealing only with "thought operations" but also with the ability to acknowledge our responsibility and to act accordingly. This is, in our view, what Puget is talking about when she speaks of making a decision.

That is why we are interested in the distinction posited by Lewkowicz between *to take the blame* and *to take responsibility*.

> Taking the blame means bearing the consequences, particularly the negative consequences, of an endeavor, whereas taking responsibility refers to the set of operations that create the subject who is able to inhabit an endeavor, be it a love, vocational, political, financial, or, I would add, therapeutic endeavor.
>
> (Lewkowicz, quoted in Puget, ibid., p. 217)

In everyday language we talk about "taking the blame." The expression "to carry the burden" emphasizes the weight of the superego dimension. Nonetheless, responsibility, in our view, is tied to the dimension of desire rather than to the order of the superego. The clinical cases described above bring us closer to the question of analysts' responsibilities. Our point of departure is the need to determine the form taken by trauma in each subject. What remains blank? How does each subject confront what cannot be symbolized? And furthermore, what subjective position did he or she occupy when the trauma occurred? Only then shall we be able to help patients reunite with their complexity, with the vicissitudes of their pain.

Through the clinical material, nourishment provided by fraternal wefts and tensions between sameness and difference introduced another dimension to the concept of responsibility. What is the fate of alienness in the fraternal weft? Joaquín can recognize himself neither in difference nor in sameness. The face, what remains blank (*en blanco*), seems to be also the target (*blanco*) of the violence he stages (see Figure 7.3). With his exposed, torn face, Joaquín finds himself before a specular image whose exteriority he cannot identify.

Something very different happened between four-year-old Gina and Mora, who established rules of coexistence through their experience of siblinghood. Hospitably committing to each other, they were able to find in their link both emotional intimacy and the ability to discriminate between them. In this case, the fate of the fraternal weft was not alienation in specularity. These girls are able to recognize difference in sameness without blurring the boundaries that separate them.

When patients seek help because they have suffered the impact of trauma, turning the listening process into a fraternal partnership may be a way of incorporating an increased operational plasticity into the creation of a clinical device. It is our responsibility to be subjectively available to contain, and also to be flexible in the delimitation of the clinical field when we are still at a stage where we do not understand what is taking place. The above discussion shows that, when viewed from a conceptual perspective, responsibility must operate as a guiding compass – as a potential indicator of diagnosis and prognosis.

We can talk about responsibility when patients become producers of subjectivity thanks to the relationship they establish with conflict. Realizing that one is responsible and acting accordingly involves working on this conflict; it means learning how to endure it, a learning experience that results from the analytic process. We agree with Levinas's definition of responsibility toward the other as "the essential primary and fundamental structure of subjectivity" (Levinas, 1985, p. 95) that puts an end to the "anonymous and senseless rumbling of being." When this author describes subjectivity in ethical terms, he claims that "being human is equivalent to not being; living humanely means doing anything for the other" (Ayuso Díez, 1985, p. 15). There would be a "deposition of sovereignty by the ego, a relationship that is devoid of inter-esse, of the attempt to preserve oneself in one's own being (*esse* in Latin)" (Levinas, ibid., p. 52).

Thus conceived, subjectivity is not autonomous; it is for others first. Subjects are responsible for others without expecting reciprocity. Such responsibility "no longer . . . belong[s] to consciousness; it is not an activating thought process put into practice, nor is it even a duty that would impose itself from without and from within." Responsibility toward the other entails "a change in the status of 'me'" (Blanchot, 1986, p. 45). Levinas unambiguously states that "the tie with the Other is knotted only as responsibility whether accepted or refused, whether knowing or not knowing how to assume it, whether able or unable to do something concrete with the Other" (Levinas, 1985, p. 97).

Freud is also categorical when he claims that loving your neighbor as yourself goes against original human nature:

> their neighbor is for them not only a potential helper or sexual object, but also someone who tempts them to satisfy their aggressiveness on him, to exploit his capacity for work without compensation, to use him sexually without his consent, to seize his possessions, to humiliate him, to cause him pain, to torture and to kill him. . . . In consequence of this primary mutual hostility of human beings, civilized society is perpetually threatened with disintegration.
>
> (Freud, 1930, pp. 58–59)

76 Couples and families today

Culture imposes alterations and restrictions on the dispositions of the drives. Fraternity, then, would appear as a conflicting tension between individual needs and/or demands, and those that result from belonging to a group. Thus, from biblical myth to contemporary modes of fratricide, there is a long process where expressions of extermination and annihilation of fellow beings intertwine with recognition, care, and responsibility for the lives of others. Responsibility builds community.

It is important to resort to the notion of shared responsibility to conceive of the mode of functioning of a relationship among peers as the construction of a solidarity network. A peer perspective is needed to repair the wounded social fabric. Thus understood, responsibility bears instituting power. It operates as a bridging concept between the fellow-being complex and the fraternal partnership.

In the cure, adopting a position of responsibility involves the ability not only to incorporate what was split but also to grant it meaning. In this sense, responsibility humanizes. It entails the projection into a possible future of horizons, trust, and hope.

Notes

1 Freud, 1895, p. 331.
2 We are not ignoring the interesting problems posed by the Freud-Ferenczi controversy in relation to the question of psychic reality. Ferenczi points out that trauma primarily represents the imposition of an alien psychic reality that is oblivious to the child's needs, added to disavowal by a significant other.
3 The authors are playing with the words *"arrebatar,"* to snatch or tear away by force, and *"arrebatado,"* used to describe the face when it is burning red.
4 Levinas, 1979, p. 89.
5 The authors use the word *"hermanar,"* derived from *hermano*, brother. There is no exact equivalent in English, that is why I translated as "bring together."

Chapter 8

Deficit and excess in contemporary life

According to Foucault,

> one of the forms – perhaps we should call them "habits" – one of the most harmful habits in contemporary thought ... [is] the analysis of the present as being precisely, in history, a present of rupture, or of high point, or of completion or of a returning dawn. .... I think we should have the modesty to say to ourselves that, on the one hand, the time we live in is not the unique or fundamental or irruptive point in history where everything is completed and begun again. We must also have the modesty to say, on the other hand, that ... the time we live in is very interesting; it needs to be analyzed and broken down, and that we would do well to ask ourselves, "What is today?"
>
> (Foucault, 1976–1988)

We are part of a generation of professionals who suffered symptoms of desubjectivation during our analytic training and professional development. To inquire into our present as psychoanalysts, we may need to evoke some milestones in our journey. We started our training by exploring the work of authors such as Berlinguer, Laing, Basaglia, Foucault, Cooper, Pichon-Rivière, and Szasz. We read *Psiquiatría y Poder* (*Psychiatry and Power*), *The Politics of Experience and the Bird of Paradise*, and *Sanity, Madness and the Family*, to mention just a few.

We are permeated by a yearning for the 1970s, when we worked in psychiatry wards from which we were expelled – "the Clínicas," headed by M. Matrajt, "the Lanús," led by M. Goldenberg and V. Baremblit, "the Avellaneda," ran by S. Berman, and so many other wards that ceased to exist during the dictatorship. Besides dismantling the public system and the country's solidarity networks, the military effected a break, a standstill in the field of mental health by fully suppressing innovating movements. Our anchor was destroyed. In our personal case, we never went back to working regularly in a hospital, and our ties to the academy were also compromised.

78 Couples and families today

It is no wonder, then, that this historical topic has not lost its relevance. When we consider public mental healthcare in Argentina today, we find huge deficiencies and limitations. We need to retrace some of the steps taken by psychoanalysis to understand current ways of processing conflict. Conversion hysteria, pathognomonic during Freud's time and characterized by paralysis, astasia-abasia, and other symptoms, appears today in other guises – it surfaces on the Internet or in pole dancing.

Camila is a very pretty 17-year-old. She is tall and thin, and dresses provocatively. She seeks help because she throws up. She has several tattoos, which she proudly flaunts. Shortly after starting treatment, coinciding with her graduation trip,[1] Camila gets involved with a young man and has sex for the first time. She feels she is falling in love.

During the first session after the trip, she tells the analyst that some pictures of her in her bra have appeared on Facebook. One night she had too much to drink at a dance club, and she climbed on a speaker and started dancing. A male friend asked her to lift her T-shirt and took some pictures. When they came back to Buenos Aires, he suggested posting the pictures on Facebook, and she thought it was very funny. When the analyst asks her if she has considered the possibility of a conflict with her boyfriend, Camila gets upset and changes the tone of the conversation. She gets mad at the analyst, complains that the analyst "doesn't understand anything," and refuses to think about the issue.

When she comes to her next hour she is very angry. She recounts that her boyfriend is furious and does not want to see her; he broke up with her with no explanation. She learned through a female friend that he had felt humiliated by the knowledge that a picture of his girlfriend with no shirt on was circulating on the Internet. Camila is outraged at her boyfriend's lack of trust. She does not believe that these photos are at all relevant. They were just a meaningless game, since she was committed to the relationship. In her own words, "In the end, what's the difference between a bikini and underwear?"

Regardless of diagnostic considerations, the question we are asking here is in what ways new communication practices are influencing the way we connect with others. The anthropologist Paula Sibilia claims that attempts to explain new phenomena that entail the public broadcast of private life as the exacerbation of an always-present latent narcissism and voyeurism are insufficient. This author suggests that a significant transformation is taking place whereby the foundations for the construction of subjectivities are shifting. The idea of an intimate world has lost validity. "In this culture of appearances, of the spectacle, of visibility . . . the world becomes, in a way, an object of design . . . the logic of visibility and the market of appearances play a critical role in the construction of the self" (Sibilia, 2008, p. 104). Avoiding anonymity and gaining visibility have become key goals.

Deficit and excess in contemporary life 79

Displaying private images on the Web is now customary, but people's perceptions of this practice differ and even oppose each other. For Camila, showing herself in her bra has no obscene connotations, while for her boyfriend it does. She takes offense at his reaction and emphasizes her faithfulness; he feels humiliated by her display. While certain practices seem to have been naturalized due to their frequency, their widespread presence is not accompanied by a homogenous discourse about them.

The idea of privacy is changing; the need to show oneself, to be looked at seems to have breached the boundaries between private and public. Gaining visibility is now a way of existing. Yet there is no radical break between the old world and the new: between the world where privacy was associated with modesty and shame, and this other one where in order to be, one must show oneself. We are currently undergoing a period of transition, and we participate in both.

Individual and group strategies that challenge hegemonic trends in the construction of the self are countless and varied. If today's social context promotes indecent exposure, psychoanalysis should aim to restore the dimension of desire. It is true that there is a tendency to externalize the private world in search of fleeting emotional experiences. Yet at the same time, the Internet has other, interesting effects, such as the fluidity of communication and new ways of being in touch through the creation of playful, creative modes of organizing and functioning.

The twenty-first century is witnessing the dissolution of the conventional profile of patients seeking analysis. Perhaps the most pressing concern is the abandonment of individual responsibility – the lack of ownership of the conflicts that constitute us. What does "subjectivity in crisis" mean? What are we talking about when we speak of new symptoms?

Throughout the twentieth century, Western society flew the banner of progress. Its ideal was to advance in every sphere. Psychoanalytic discourse goes in a different direction. It does not call for progress in the sense of success, but for a responsible subjectivity that can account for its experience. In his lecture on "Patologías de la ética" ("Pathologies of Ethics"), Miller (1991) defines responsibility based on accountability. Irresponsible people cannot account for their acts, and hence decisions are left in the hands of the Other. In these pathologies, subjects claim that they cannot help themselves; their responsibility has been eclipsed (Tarrab, 2009). In this sense, psychoanalysis always has a disturbing effect, for it demands an ethics of responsibility rather than the ethics of surrender and disavowal promoted by contemporary culture.

We live harassed and oppressed by the naturalization of the abuse perpetrated by stimuli and cultural injunctions that draw us away even from ourselves. There are no adequate norms in place to address transgression. Impunity and violence are now legitimate modes of expression. Psychic

80 Couples and families today

failure seems to have become the common factor in psychopathological complaints. As Agamben well states,

> just as modern man has been deprived of his biography, his experience has likewise been expropriated. . . . It is this non-translatability of experience that now makes everyday existence intolerable – as never before – rather than an alleged poor quality of life or its meaninglessness compared with the past.
>
> (Agamben, 1993, pp. 13 and 14)

Ariel, aged 16, started therapy with a sense of despondency and no expectation of improvement. After having been prescribed Ritalin for two years, he was convinced that the "solution" for his suffering could only be encapsulated in a drug. The patient profile outlined in the interviews highlighted both an attitude of "fluttering around" – sampling things here and there without delving into anything – and a difficulty to go deeper into projects and/or undertakings and sustain them over time. His life as a student was frustrating because his performance failed to meet academic requirements. He had been diagnosed with ADD despite not having been thoroughly examined.

This young man lived surrounded by electronic gadgets and screens that allowed him to be online eight to eleven hours a day. Text messages, Facebook, WhatsApp, Netflix, and the PlayStation were his interlocutors. Yet despite his inability to cling to anything (with the complications such inability involves), there were some textbooks with which he did identify. He also had a sleeping disorder (he slept four or five hours a day), and his irritability and bad mood were prevalent. He lived against the current of his family, shutting himself away in his "bunker." His relationship with his parents and siblings had significantly deteriorated. He had been stigmatized as "the ADD child," and was experiencing his adolescence from this marginalized place.

Kovadloff and Tesone (2002) discuss the consequences of the increasingly common use of drugs in mental health:

> The discovery and use of psychothropic drugs has certainly been a major step forward in the follow-up and evolution of seriously disturbed patients since 1952. . . . No skilled observer, however, can overlook the fact that professionals are currently committing damaging excesses. The pharmaceutical industry is bent on influencing diagnostic processes by introducing a therapeutic logic that subjects psychiatrists to constant pressure. Practitioners are enticed to rapidly suppress symptoms as if this were the ultimate therapeutic goal, instead of viewing them as the essential preliminary requirement for patients to feel that they play the leading role in their treatment.
>
> (Kovadloff and Tesone, 2002)

Due to their configuration, intensive use of computers trains us to carry out several activities simultaneously. The logic of disjunction with which we learned to think and operate has lost power over our thought processes. Multitasking does away with dilemmas (either A or B); the logic of conjunction predominates (A is possible and B is also possible). Curiously, psychological complaints related to attention deficit, difficulty to focus, and distraction have become more and more frequent, not only among children but also among adults. This coincidence, however, does not explain attention disorders. What concerns those of us who grew up with the motto of "one thing at a time" is the question of what we lose and what we gain by opening so many windows simultaneously.

The pathologies that bring patients to our offices share common features: a disturbing symbolic deficit, the prevalence of action language, and marks that are typical of the devastation produced by automatic anxiety. Addiction, bulimia and anorexia, the self-cutting syndrome, and panic attacks are some of the clinical manifestations of impulsiveness. The instatement of disavowal as the major defense mechanism, the increasing fragility of links, desubjectivization processes, and the enshrinement of the instant, all prevailing features of present-day society, lead us to believe that paradigms have changed.

We live in an age that favors existential inconsistency. There is an imperative to be happy accompanied by narratives that lack density. New symptoms have emerged due to the loss of values and ideals and of role models imbued with authority (Tarrab, 2009). From a psychoanalytic perspective, we cannot disengage ourselves subjectively from the times we live in. Rather, we must stay alert to their excesses and deficits, which are two sides of the same coin.

We are committed to a clinical practice where subjectivization is the result of a desiring position. Our responsibility, and our stance as analysts, is to support with our discourse the metaphor and the manifold voices of the erotic and vital aspects of humanness. It is in the context of analytic work that new places can be created, unprecedented potencies opened, and questions posed. We find ourselves faced with a paradox; our practice and its ethics go against the grain of the mechanisms imposed by present-day culture.

Note

1 In Argentina it is customary for high school seniors to travel for a week to celebrate their graduation.

Chapter 9

Exploring memory and forgetting

> *In these processes it particularly often happens that something is "remembered" which could never have been "forgotten" because it was never at any time noticed – was never conscious.*
>
> Sigmund Freud[1]

Memory as construction

Few topics in psychoanalysis can be approached from as many perspectives as memory. We should doubtlessly start with childhood amnesia, where many of the marks that will determine the course of our life are inscribed. At the same time, memory and remembering, as a form of working-through, refer us to the foundations of psychoanalytic technique.

What is worth remembering? How can we curb the conquering will of memory, which aims to inventory everything, to retain and accumulate? When people seek our help, we get ready to listen. We urge them to relinquish what they know – to let go, if possible, of a scenario that, being revisited so often, has become fixed, like a still image. Patients tend to come to analysis accompanied by such indelible scripts.

> "Funes the Memorious," one of Borges' best-known stories, has become the obligatory guest whenever we discuss the question of remembering. Irineo Funes obstinately insists on describing events by reproducing them with absolute accuracy. He skips nothing. He perfectly replicates yesterday's sunset. He does not screen or choose; he accumulates. Rather than of congestion of the lungs, says Pontalis (2012), Funes died of congestion of memory. Funes's memory is suffocating; it died before being born. If memory's goal is to be a faithful copy, Pontalis adds, it cannot be a vital force.

We believe that when we no longer associate it with the static preservation of an already constituted knowledge and reveal it as a construction,

Exploring memory and forgetting   83

as a moving process, we can look at memory in a different way.[2] We envision it free of its ties to the past in order to think of it as a construction of the present. There would be no memory, states Virno (2015), if memory were not, above all, about the present. When we remember we go back to a place we had never visited.

At the same time, when Freud (1912a) claims that analysts must carry out a feat of memory, he emphasizes the significance of patients' inscription in the analyst's memory. There is, therefore, a capital of shared memory in the patient-analyst link that begins to grow from the start of the treatment. Focusing on signifying elements during the work of the transference and bringing them to mind is the task of the analyst. As they listen, analysts cut, interpret, underline the material. Their memory does not work as a storing archive. Rather, it highlights signifiers, points out recurrences, articulates patients' discourses; it has the effect of an interpretation.

Memory operates in the field of psychoanalytic practice in such a way that it produces an event. It introduces something unprecedented. As Freud writes to Fliess in 1896,

> the material present in the form of memory traces [is] being subject from time to time to a re-arrangement in accordance with fresh circumstances – to a re-transcription. Thus what is essentially new about my theory is the thesis that memory is present not once but several times over, that it is laid down in various species of indications.
>
> (Masson, 1985, p. 207)

Transference neurosis develops in the here and now of the link. The transference space in the present is the scene of memory in the analysis. According to Derrida (1978), when we ponder memory in a dimension that transcends remembering, we instate it as the writing pad of subjectivity. The psychic text is not a simple archive containing unambiguous marks; it is rewritten time and again, and every new writing shapes, and is shaped by, earlier ones.

As Freud (1925) asserts in "A Note upon the 'Mystic Writing Pad,'" memories constitute a potential destination for memory traces inscribed in our wax slate. In reality, adds J.-B. Pontalis, memories act as a screen for memory, even though they pretend to correspond to experiences deposited in it that survived the erosion of time. Whether we are dealing with screen memories or falsified memories, "there is in general no guarantee of the data produced by our memory" (Freud, 1899, p. 315).

This statement brings to light the fact that memory is biased and fragmentary, and that it is influenced by the drives. Forgetfulness reveals both the persistency and the lacunar quality of our childhood memories,

84 Couples and families today

and how they emerge later in a distorted fashion. According to May and Mauer (2003, p. 92),

> Building the writing pad is the work of analysis. What psychoanalysis writes down is the ability to rewrite every time. The clear, receptive surface of the analytic device offers those who demand analysis the ability to come into contact with their marks and reorganize them in the light of the present.

When the analytic scene is multi-personal, listening broadens. A *joint free narrative* (to differentiate it from free association) and the mise en scène of the transference activate and enhance both evocation and forgetting. Subjects' memory is contained in, and intertwines with, the memories of others in the manner of a stained glass, cut and colored by the subjectivity of each participant. There is a unique unconscious selection of what is remembered and what is forgotten.

The myths of origin of a couple, family, group, or institution demand that *memory* weave a fabric with memories that both screen and reveal. In the context of analytic work, these memories acquire the quality of the *après-coup*, thus facilitating the emergence of new and diverse views. Anecdotes recounted from different perspectives by the members of a link show this interplay not only of memories but also of forgotten experiences.

Patients will gradually compose their history by resorting to family life scenes, stories, flavors, anecdotes, childhood fears, and other images from the album of time. Yet such composition is never final. Even without having access to, or full control over, the archive and its traces, if we are willing to remember, as Aulagnier (1991) said so well, we can gradually construct the past in order to move toward the future.

From clinical practice: constructing memory

Javier seeks help due to a situation that causes him anxiety but he's unable to solve. He claims he is deeply in love with his lover but gets along very well with his wife. He does not want to leave her and their children. Coming from a very religious family, he goes to church often and attends spiritual retreats. He is a practicing Catholic and feels at fault in relation to a sacrament of the Church.

Javier mentions a character in a book with whom he claims to identify. This character is hypocritical, has many faces, is a forger by trade. The patient says he has been wondering why he never moved from his childhood neighborhood. He bought a house two blocks away from where his grandparents used to live, and his store is also nearby.

Exploring memory and forgetting   85

Analyst: "Everything within a few blocks?"

Javier: "What is more, there's a tree there that is my childhood tree, a tree I planted. A neighbor still brings me fruit from that tree. Why didn't I leave the neighborhood?"

He associates that this tree is very important because his father used to say that it was "very sickly," very weak, and he bet his father that the tree would grow. Now he reaps the fruit.

Analyst: "The tree is there, and it grew . . ."

Javier: "You say, 'The tree is there, and it grew,' but to me the tree isn't important. It's the fruit that's important."

Analyst: "Why is the fruit so important?"

Javier: "Well, maybe I can't get a divorce because of my children, because the children are the fruit. And I'm tied to my family, to the branches of the tree and its fruit . . . the family web."

Analyst: "Then the fruit is more important than the tree?"

Sometimes he regretfully tells the analyst that he has forgotten what they discussed in earlier sessions. Then he apologizes, opens his briefcase, and takes out a notebook where he writes things down. He records his conclusions. At the same time, he claims he does not know if he is capable of doing anything new. Javier has not realized yet that what he is doing with his memory represents a radical undertaking; a memory created in analysis inscribes something new.

On forgetting

We consider that forgetting is a tool of memory. Far from being an obstacle to our work, it acts as a compass that helps us identify both memories that resist revelation and protective forgetting, that is, forgetting that is at the service of memory. The fact that we need to forget redeems the notion of forgetting from its well-founded bad press – from the idea that forgetting constitutes a form of silencing that seems suspicious and arouses mistrust. We believe that what has been forgotten has a raison d'être, a role, and it is in analysis where it finds a significant opportunity to acquire meaning.

Forgetting is the condition of possibility of remembering; we must forget in order to remember. Something that was never conscious "could never have been 'forgotten' because it was never at any time noticed" (Freud, 1914, p. 149). Undergoing analysis means becoming someone who remembers, someone who constructs one's memory – the memory of what was forgotten and the memory of what needs to be inscribed.

86 Couples and families today

Oblivion in Greek means "no mark." We might also define it as unrecorded mark. Pontalis (2003) argues that it is what never occurred that is repeated. Since it never happened, it did not exist as an event; it remained outside the text. In other words, the challenge posed by memory in the clinical field is its demand that we resort to both forgetting and remembering. Moreover, in relation to the memory itself, which, as Freud rightly emphasizes, is always a screen memory, we are interested in the production emerging from psychic work in the transference.

Forgetting, J.-B. Pontalis will add, is necessary to grant density to experienced time. A memory that is conceived of as timeless is a dead memory. A living memory requires forgetting. There would hence be two types of forgetting: the one determined by unconscious resistance, at the service of concealment, and the one that, by operating at the service of memory, contributes to keeping it alive.

Romanovich Luria studied two cases that have become classic in psychiatric literature. One of the patients was a man who had been wounded by a bullet during World War II and had lost his memory and his ability to remember. With great effort, he strived to retrieve shreds of his memory in order to maintain a connection with life. On the other end of the spectrum, Romanovich Luria refers to the "mnemonist," who had shown a prodigious memory since childhood. He could not forget, and neither could he read; he had no room for new texts. The Russian psychiatrist claimed that both the man who could not remember and the mnemonist suffered from an illness. "Many of us are anxious to find ways to improve our memories; none of us how to deal with the problem of how to forget" (Luria, 1968, p. 67).

In his lecture on forgetting Yerushalmi asks a compelling question: "Given the need both to remember and to forget, where are the lines to be drawn?" (Yerushalmi, 1988, p. 107, 1991). In a sense, psychoanalysis has a faithful, committed relationship with both memory and forgetting, which contribute the raw materials for psychoanalytic work. Memory is always entwined with forgetting, with which it necessarily coexists. It is by way of forgetting, moreover, that memories gain consistency. Each author performs selective cuts; each of us, not knowing why, chooses, gives shape to, and imprints memories in a unique way.

Producing a forgetful person is likely to be the first great challenge to psychoanalysis. It involves the deconstruction of those cuts, performed on memories, that served to create patients' history. De-totalized memory is, in fact, memory that has been reorganized in such a way that new meanings emerge. Forgetting means yielding to the reconstructing power of memory rather than to the effort to retain past experiences.

Ricoeur provides a detailed discussion of the phenomenology of forgetting that we have found useful to establish the vantage point from where we want to approach this complex issue. This author suggests a typology that distinguishes, among others, a mode of forgetting that he calls "impeded memory," which is the memory of the unconscious.

He also considers other forms of forgetting, such as manipulated memory, which refers to the inevitable cuts and selectivity involved in any narrative. "The space of memory," claims Elizabeth Jelin,

> is . . . an arena of political struggle. . . . Slogans such as "memory against oblivion" or "against silence" hide an opposition between distinct and rival memories (each one with its own forgetfulness). In truth, what is at stake is an opposition of "memory against memory."
>
> (Jelin, 2003, p. xviii)

Finally, Ricoeur refers to "commanded" or institutional forgetting, which corresponds to an agreed-upon forgetting, the forgetting of amnesty. Out of all these categories, we will only look at the memory of the unconscious.

The work of construction of memory and forgetting in analytic work, states Moreno, seeks to promote the emergence of

> what was left out of the biography . . . in a transference present illuminated by the flashing of broken memories. . . . What interests us in an analysis is the return of the non-repressed, of those aspects of experience that the associative functioning of psychic counting could not catalogue.
>
> (Moreno, 2010, pp. 22 and 26)

From clinical practice: instances of remembering and forgetting

María, aged 22, who is in her fourth year of analysis, had an accident a few months ago. The horse she was riding bolted; it started running out of control until she fell and hit her head. She lost consciousness due to a concussion, which caused a vestibular condition that was compensated by way of rehabilitation. A few weeks earlier she had met Gustavo, a young man with whom she established a love relationship. Gustavo had fallen from a scaffold shortly before meeting her. He had survived because he had landed on a canvass awning.

When María was 17 she traveled to Spain, the home of her ancestors. There she met and fell in love with Eulogio, a young man who was a few years her senior. The day before María's return to Argentina Eulogio died in an accident. While accidents insist as a signifier, the young woman resists any association related to her fall, which she considers "just a random event." "Not everything can be interpreted," she claims.

A few months later María comes to a session in the evening, which is unusual. She says it is the first time she has noticed that there is a parking

88 Couples and families today

garage across the street from the analyst's office. She cannot believe it has always been there. Then she mentions that she feels pressured by her boyfriend, who repeatedly asks her if she is truly committed to the relationship. In a tone of concern, she adds that he has told her of several episodes where his life was at risk. "With Eulogio's accident I've had more than enough," she states.

"The anniversary of Eulogio's death was one or two months ago, right?" the analyst asks, as if thinking aloud. The patient gives the exact date. Then the analyst asks yet another question: "And when was your accident with the horse?" After a brief silence, María answers, "You've left me speechless. The thing with the . . . horse was the day after the anniversary." She recalls thinking about Eulogio before getting on the horse. She knew that back in his home country, they had said a prayer in his memory the day before.

We believe that remembering in the transference gives memories a different status, a new inscription. The memory that is brought to analysis is taken apart and rebuilt with a different configuration; it is deconstructed, reduced, and expanded, all at the same time. With our interventions, we introduce a way of thinking that probes into patients' memory and makes room for the construction of a new perspective.

Notes

1 Freud, 1914, p. 149.
2 Nietzsche (1874) stated that nineteenth-century human beings suffered from a historical illness due to surplus knowledge and consciousness of history. They were no longer capable of creating and making true history, as creating requires forgetting.

Chapter 10

Sexualities in the plural
Conflicting practices and representations

Sexual heterogeneities under the microscope of the sexuality device

During the modern era, besides the "alliance devices" that governed (conjugal and parental) family exchanges, the West invented the sexuality device. Each era designs and regulates new ways of processing and experiencing sexuality that involve specific codes, symptoms, and modes of interpretation. Sexuality, therefore, is a socio-historical construction.

Foucault (1978) claims that rather than restricting it, the *"mise en discours"* ("putting into discourse") of sex – the explosion of discourses about sex that characterized the last three centuries – set in motion a mechanism of increasing incitement. Power techniques applied to sex have promoted the dissemination and implantation of polymorphous sexualities. This author emphatically points to the relationship between sexuality and power. He includes these heterogeneous sexualities within the sexuality device, which is intended to penetrate and control the individual and social bodies. It is thanks to this device that heterogeneities would seek to become "normal" and to be absorbed, in the end, by the device itself. In this way, the sexuality device achieves effects of homogeneity and conspires against the non-conformist, opposition power of sexual diversities. "What does the appearance of all these peripheral sexualities signify?" asks Foucault.

> Is the fact that they could appear in broad daylight a sign that the scale had become more lax? Or does the fact that they were given so much attention testify to a stricter regime and its concern to bring them under close supervision?
>
> (Foucault, 1978, p. 40)

A patient relates: "I talked a lot with . . . I visited my friend Gabriel, I told you about him last year, my friend from acting class. Well, now he's Ivanna; he started dressing as a woman and changed his name. Gabriel,

90 Couples and families today

who is now Ivanna, told me . . ." In this patient's discourse, a man's ability to adopt a woman's name and dress in women's clothes seems to have become normal. Is transgender ceasing to be a peripheral sexuality, as it was in Foucault's analysis?

Less than forty years ago the French philosopher talked about an explosion of heterogeneous sexualities and their heretic power. Today we are witnessing the appearance of legal frameworks that regulate and legitimate these sexualities. In 2012 the Argentine legislature passed the Gender Identity Act, whereby people over 18 years of age can change their record information. They can rectify their name and sex on their birth certificate and on their national identity document. This law defines gender identity as

> the internal, individual experience of gender as it is felt by each person, which may or may not correspond to the sex assigned at birth. . . . It may involve changes in appearance or bodily functions through pharmacological, surgical, or other procedures, as long as these have been freely chosen.[1]

Every right is a social gain that is secured by overcoming resistance. A variety of social and political factors gradually created the conditions of possibility for new laws to be passed. We wonder whether these laws imply the broadening of the boundaries of tolerance – a better coexistence with diversity.

Multiple contemporary discourses "make sex talk." Diversity resists traditional definitions constructed on the basis of a binary framework (Fernández, 2012). Facebook has recently announced that it will offer its users fifty options for gender identification. The drop-down menu that appears in the Basic Information tab includes personalized, non-binary options such as intersex, agender/neutrois, androgynous, gender fluid, gender nonconforming/variant, genderqueer, and neither (Ball, 2014; Weber, 2011). Let us look at a few brief clinical vignettes that illustrate the various representations of sexuality that are currently circulating in Argentine society.

"I'm the only one of my friends who still hasn't had sex," says Martina, who is 22 years old. "When we get together, I have nothing to talk about. If you're a virgin at this age it sucks, they look at you strangely." It seems as if sexuality were a social demand; one must practice it so as not to be excluded, so as to be part of the group.

"I made out with Pablo," says Guillermina, who is 16 years old. "It was great, I didn't feel anything." Emotions seem to have lost value. It is indifference that is appreciated – the disconnection between sex and feelings.

"How do you get into the touch-and-go[2] circuit?" wonders Eliana, aged 38. She states that she wants encounters that promise sex without intimacy – that will not involve her emotionally or take too much of her time. A "touch-and-go" that will "solve the sexuality issue for me."

Sexualities in the plural 91

In these clinical vignettes sexuality appears as a categorical imperative. In addition, to show the manifold differing and conflicting discursivities, we would like to mention the emergence of a particular type of group. An 18-year-old young man created an online community, the Asexual Visibility and Education Network (AVEN), which condemns the central role of sexuality in our culture. Members of this community argue that in a society that believes in the essential nature of sex, a person who is not interested in sexuality seems like a non-person. They seek to unmask, to denaturalize the imperative of sexuality.

Adolescent sexualities today

It is hard to understand the current socio-historical context that cannot be mapped by resorting to the reference points that had supported us as analysts in the past. Juana, aged 15, tells her analyst that during the weekend's *"previa"*[3] at a friend's place, the six closest female friends in the group locked themselves in the bathroom to make out because they were curious about the others' technique. Then they discussed what each had done: if they opened their mouth too much, if their way of hugging was unique, or who was the most enthusiastic. What concerned Juana was not that the experience had involved girls but that she might have cheated on her new boyfriend.

If something has dramatically changed in recent years in adolescents' behavior, it is the range of manifestations of sexuality. The adult gaze rates the sexuality of puberty as precocious; the adults take for granted that the search for pleasure is focused on intercourse, when in reality this search seems to have become an extension of the *polymorphously perverse disposition* typical of infantile sexuality. Excitations and satisfaction are not associated with a genital encounter with another. We must thoroughly revisit these sexual practices, which tend to be viewed from both a metapsychological and a contextual perspective, as increasingly precocious in relation to the exogamic exit.

According to Foucault, the sexuality device revolves around the "grip on bodies and their materiality, their forces, energies, sensations and pleasures," and power is the organizing force. Sex is not an autonomous agency. Conversely, it is "the most speculative, most ideal, and most internal element in a deployment of sexuality organized by power" (Foucault, 1978, p. 155). Furthermore, it has strong standardizing effects on the economic exploitation of erotization; bodies must be thin, beautiful, and tanned (Castro, 2011).

Among adolescents, certain practices performed on the body have transformed it into the main site where subjectivity becomes visible. These practices entail a way of making oneself seen, of embodying that differs greatly from the classic female hystericization that we witnessed as we grew up and trained. It is no longer repression that fences sexuality in. There are other forms of control that affect it.

Emotional dams such as shame and revulsion do not operate in the same way in online exchanges than in personal contacts. New codes that regulate how we make ourselves seen on the Web coexist with other modes of approach and meeting that are more challenging in that they are face to face. The main goal behind online exchanges is to be sustained by the other's gaze – what Sibilia (2008) calls alter-directed sexuality. The ultimate purpose is not to show or share but to gauge the effect of the performance. On this equation – how many look and approve (how many "likes" one gets) – depends our self-esteem.

Alcohol tends to be the justification both for libidinal slips, facilitated by lenient Internet codes, and for the weakening of the inhibitions that accompany bodily contact. Increasing use of social networks has generated new modes of seduction and interaction with others. The ability to be with someone online without the need for his or her factual presence encourages young people to behave without modesty in some cases, or to conceal their fears of personal contact in others.

Irina, aged 15, spends all her free time online. In the first interview she defines herself as pansexual. Her parents have brought her because she was held back a year at school. She lives in a computer world, and her only interlocutors are the members of the community of Internet users and the creators of animé cartoon series.[4] She is a highly talented illustrator and is developing an animated video game whose characters and scripts emphasize diversity (see Figure 10.1).

The game combines reality and fantasy, and would be rated G. The characters are expressive and display emotional interactions that show Irina's need to provide evidence of the unlimited combinations of sex and gender. "I advocate for the destruction of gender roles," she claims. Her love relationships and friendships unfold solely online. Curiously, her narrative concerning some of her bonds is romantic but she has not been face to face with or touched any of her intimate partners.

As Glocer Fiorini (2010) rightly argues, current social discourses and practices in the Western world are traversed by sex and gender blends and combinations. In some cases, sexuality is exercised outside heterosexual norms. Among these cases are transsexuality and transgender, which involve the rejection of normative gender assignments and codes.

Family configurations

The family model is mutating. Challenges to the paternal order, the emancipation of women, children's rebellion, and the legitimization of same-sex relationships have generated changes in the way families are formed. Yet despite its transformations, the family is still the prevailing

mode of human organization. More or less functional, more or less flexible families create highly heterogeneous filiation variants. Family photos show different landscapes. The family puzzle has become more complex. The family has become decentered; the patriarchal mark that constituted its backbone and organized it as a vertical structure has lost relevance. Extended and single-parent families are some of the examples of an increasing plurality.

Given the challenges to the idea of structure, we wonder about the fate of the family, which had been the constitutive core of subjectivity to date. The fragmentation of family life increases both the freedom and the exposure of family members. The level of autonomy and of neglect of others that we witness in its dynamics makes us hesitate to keep calling the family "nuclear." The fact is that while this institution is still a vital form of organization, at least for the moment, its mode of functioning is neither homogeneous nor univocal. The family is represented and presented as the weave of a relational weft that must be built and deciphered individually, with relational codes that vary widely even within the same social environment.

96 Couples and families today

In the family's makeup and relational dynamics we find interpersonal ties that are more flexible and freer than they used to be. At the same time, however, we see in our consultation rooms disintegrated, wounded families with unstable, fragile, and weak links. Generational differences and boundaries between functions have become blurred, and words have generally lost relevance or been left behind as a form of communication. What follows is a short illustrative vignette.

Mabel, aged seven, introduces herself to the analyst by saying, "You know I'm adopted? My mom couldn't have a baby in her belly, and so she asked a girl to make a baby for her, the girl made it and then my mom went to get me."[5] In this narrative about adoption there is an allusion to a gestation that does not include a man; a woman ordered a baby from another woman. The child has created her own theories. The hypotheses she has developed to answer questions about sexuality, origin, and the difference between the sexes are marked by current discourses. Saying that a woman ordered a baby from another woman is possible because material conditions enable women to have children without the presence of a man. Not every family involves a heterosexual couple. New reproductive technologies allow us to procreate without sexuality. The argument that homosexuality undermines the survival of the species is no longer valid.

Moreover, current configurations of adult couples evince new ways of understanding and practicing love and sexuality. Traditional relationships coexist with a range of alternatives that show a certain weakening of monogamy and of sexual exclusiveness. Open marriages, online love, and cyber-sex are some examples of encounters and failed encounters.[6] Family organization diversifies, but new types coexist with traditional ones where the nuclear family is still a valid mode of organization.

C. Soler claims that the twentieth century witnessed the appearance of a new tolerance regarding sexuality. According to this author, "in terms of sexual jouissance, everything that is not impossible is currently allowed; not only allowed, but also performed" (Soler, 2000, p. 127). Nevertheless, she considers that one boundary still remains, and that is mutual consent. Both partners must agree.

McDougall (1995), in turn, refers to heterosexualities and homosexualities as love choices and erotic practices that can configure neurotic, perverse, or delirious psychotic links. At the same time, she defines as perversion sexual relations that are imposed by an individual on another who does not consent to them (rape) or who is not responsible for his or her decisions, that is, children or mentally disturbed adults.

Finally, S. Bleichmar, faithful to her idea of psychoanalytic theory's failure to explain new modes of practicing sexuality, seeks to reposition the concept of perversion with regard to an ethics of the fellow being that overcomes incestuous and lethal jouissance. This author redefines perversion as a process characterized by the desubjectivation of the other. The body of the other is appropriated as an object deprived of subjectivity. "In this sense, perversion may accompany both the homosexual and the heterosexual object choices, as long as the subject ignores or destroys the other's subjectivity" (Bleichmar, 2010, p. 97).

Bleichmar also shows the need to consider the Oedipus complex, whatever the guises it may take across history, as an organizer of the patterns of exchange between adults and children, starting, as did Laplanche, from

98   Couples and families today

the essential asymmetry between the two. She refers to the ways in which each culture sets boundaries to the appropriation of children's bodies as a locus for adult jouissance (Bleichmar, ibid.).

These three authors, who have developed distinctive theories, share the conviction that some key psychoanalytic concepts must be redefined. The fact is that present-day psychoanalysis does not hold a unified view; different theories coexist. Fernández (2007) points out the need to deconstruct conceptual standards and moral criteria. This author warns about the risks we run when we naturalize certain viewpoints. We should develop and implement conceptual and methodological categories that allow us to operate with sex and gender diversities.

Conflicting representations and practices in relation to sexuality

Does the rise of sexual heterogeneity imply a greater social acceptance of it? It would seem that conflicting discourses, legal frameworks, and practices coexist. A few years ago two lesbian women had a son who was conceived by one of them through IVF with sperm from a sperm bank. Both consider themselves his mother. When the boy started preschool, the couple had disagreements that led to their separation. In the aftermath, the biological mother denied that her son had two mothers. While she acknowledged her homosexuality, she dismissed the idea that her son should remain outside the norm. She decided to forbid her ex-partner to contact the son. While back then there was no precedent set to protect the adoptive mother, she was able to secure visitation rights after an intense struggle. This is an example of the coexistence of conflicting representations and practices within a single person.

Even though reproduction is no longer the raison d'être of these alliances, it is clear that new modes of family organization still require the protection of the state. New regulations must be developed with regard to children's upbringing so as to safeguard adoptive parents and children. Argentina's current same-sex marriage act allows both spouses to register children as their own. Social practices, however, progress faster than theories and laws, and pose new challenges. Iara, aged 16, is advocating for the right to identity of children born through assisted reproductive technology. There is still no answer for her concern.

Posing some questions

What is the role of eroticism, sensuality, and the enigmatic, of repression and desire? How does castration operate today? Where there is power, states Foucault, there is also resistance to power. Resistance, moreover, is never in a position of exteriority; it is inside the network. Absolute control is impossible. In the face of new modes of domination, new modes of resistance will emerge. Tension does not disappear. The tendency toward normalization and control, the strife to produce homogeneity effects is ongoing, and points of resistance shift and transform. Philosophical, anthropological, and sociological developments may help generate new perspectives.

We are living in times of marked transition. We are part of the scene. We are affected as subjects and analysts by that "multiplicity of force relations immanent in the sphere in which they operate" (Foucault, 1978, p. 92). Our practice is traversed by the instituting modes of our times. How do we critically question our reference points, our pillars of support? We need to take distance from both prejudice and the unreflecting repetition of fashionable discourses. Our challenge is daring to revisit, deconstruct, and decenter hegemonic concepts in order to create new devices and, at the same time, being able to acknowledge and assume our own conflicting representations. In other words, we need to question our heritage to facilitate its transformation.

Notes

1 Law 26.743, available at www.infoleg.gov.ar/infolegInternet/anexos/195000-199999/197860/norma.htm.
2 "Touch and go" is in English in the original.
3 A get together before the evening outing. At these gatherings, teenagers get drunk before going to a club.
4 Animé is a Japanese animation technique.
5 We are grateful to Lic. Liana Ubaldini for contributing this vignette.
6 De Cristoforis (2009) discusses other models, such as singletons (couples that do not live together), metroflexibles (who have sexual relations with both men and women), swingers (groups of couples that swap partners), DINKS (double-income, no kids), polyamory (neologism that means having a steady love relationship with several people at the same time), online couples, and contingent couples (they meet every now and then for a sexual and emotional relationship).

Part II

Facing clinical challenges

Chapter 11

The psychoanalyst's writing process

I

Writing is a way of coming closer to others and sharing with them – of becoming visible. Writing, says Argentine poet Roberto Juarroz (1991), is letting others see. Every text is a means of expression and also of communication, because it needs another person, a reader, to reach a state of completeness. It is an act of self-affirmation that enables writers to develop a sense of their own existence.

The act of creating is a psychic movement that brings into play primary psychic processes that form the organizing core of theoretical or literary work. It could be argued that it is the unspeakable that provides the impetus for writing – not what has been silenced, but the "center," the unbound, the unutterable. The word plays an allusive role that preserves the dimension of the unsayable. "There is an unyielding silence in the written word," says Kovadloff (1993, p. 138). This silence, he adds, does not allude to the word that is missing but to what is missing in the word, that is, to the dissonance between word and concept.

Writing, whether literary or scientific, is intended to share meaning. It may contain, moreover, an implicit desire to endure, to transcend, but also to give testimony. From this perspective, the written word is one of the most effective ways of fighting against the isolation of silence. Jorge Luis Borges (1984) claims that words contain both expression and allusion, and are both the material and the tool with which we build a shelter that protects us from vulnerability.

The creative act is the final link in a chain, and is a constituting value of the human condition. Subjects undergo different instances of disorganization involving the disintegration of established structures that are then innovatively recreated. To create is to open up spaces, to propose something whose essence lies in difference, and to produce alternative meanings that had not existed before. This act of transgression, of challenging the established order will inevitably result in mental turmoil. Enríquez (1989) states that we often confuse death with the negative, but the latter

104 Facing clinical challenges

has two different sides. One is the destruction of life, and the other, the destruction of unity-identity, which represents a love of diversity.

Language has a dual role. First, it creates the illusion of closing the gap between word and thing (a world of meaning could slip through it). Second, creative language strives to restore the complexity of things (there is, in fact, no word that can perfectly encapsulate the intricacy of meaning). Language has an allusive quality; it involves mourning the loss of the illusion that we can gain full knowledge of ourselves and of others. Accessing the symbolic constitutes an attempt to reencounter and, simultaneously, reconstruct the object. Words have both ontological and evocative value.

Writing also performs a dual function. By means of the written word, subjects try to affirm their unambiguous presence. The text itself, however, is a metaphor. As subjects begin to write, while their original intention may have been to suggest a single meaning, their words can be interpreted in many ways. Those who write are but the creators of the text; they do not control its fate. No writer is immune to this threatening and rending mourning process. Paradoxical though it may seem, there is nothing that triggers such an array of interpretations as a written text.

Those who have made the journey from inspiration to production will agree that the writing process involves a series of different stages. At the outset, the writer's mind is focused on a concern, a question or idea that has long sought expression. Usually, these ideas appear spontaneously (the writer had not actively searched for them) and refuse to go away. The beginning of the writing process is not necessarily a pleasurable experience. On occasion, writers are overcome by the pressing, inescapable need to formulate certain concepts in a specific way. According to Juarroz (1991), this experience generates great tension and draws on all our mental skills and emotional sensibilies.

A flash of inspiration sparks our initial enthusiasm. Yet when faced with an insurmountable block, we will likely seek refuge in reading, searching for citations from other authors who will become part of our work as fragments of text between quotation marks. In this way, we borrow from writers whose work has already been thought through and published. Taking shelter in this haven of citations, writers can protect themselves from overwhelming confusion, helplessness, and paralysis. At times, our curiosity and the desire to write fade in view of the absolute certainty that everything has already been said and there is no place for other hypotheses and concepts. Authors become extremely self-critical. If any new ideas do emerge, they are immediately dismissed as being fallacious and of little interest.

Only after having crossed this territory, fraught with obstacles and pitfalls that are a source of great anxiety, can original questions and ideas resurface. A spark, a glimmer of a notion heralds the possibility of devising new hypotheses, of starting the creative act, of crafting ideas and concepts so that we can slowly abandon the safety of quotation marks. Writing requires patience; authors must work through initial feelings of inadequacy and lack of inspiration to tap the richness of their creative potential.

It is important to differentiate between two kinds of writing. The first is little more than the impersonal act of copying down a piece of discourse onto paper. One person records what another person says, like the mechanical transcription of a scribe. In this case, the text reproduces the meaning of another writer. In contrast, the written word can be used as a means for the expression of the writer's own concepts. When writing involves describing and exploring uncharted territory, authors can break free from the constraints of idealization and begin the struggle to find their own words. When this is the case, there are always omissions and unanswered questions; the intended meaning will never be fully clear.

Writing produces a lack, an absence or insufficiency. In their search for possible meanings, writers seek to populate an empty space. Nevertheless, ideas do not always fit neatly into the words that express them.

> My hand almost always obeys me. When I write, however, I lose control over the shapes I trace. When rereading my notes and thinking about what I wanted to express, I usually find myself at fault concerning style and coherence, if not spelling.
>
> (Pommier, 1996, p. 7)

II

When analysts go from the domain of clinical experience to the realm of writing, they change places in relation to the spoken word (the usual means of communication in clinical practice). Through the writing process, analysts' own subjectivity can unfold; there is a search for a different space where to process and analyze the verbal discourse of the consulting room, which is treated in the strictest confidence. Paradoxically, they find shelter in writing. The written word is both cathartic and therapeutic. Analysts leave the prescribed privacy of the consulting room and move into the public domain. Such exposure grants visibility to their work. It provides a dimension of public intelligibility to what was originally private, and allows them to achieve a certain degree of self-legitimization.

The written form demands both consistency and coherence. Over the course of the writing process, analysts cross out and correct while assessing and questioning their own professional training and their approach to clinical work. Thus, writing is also a means of "self-supervision." Analysts' written work is rarely a dispassionate exploration of a phenomenon. Rather, the content reveals the problems they are facing at that particular moment of their career and the position they take in the face of the questions emerging from their practice. We could even go as far as to say that every text is a sort of professional autobiography. As André Green states, "The act of writing is a strange act, as unnecessary as it is unpredictable, but for the writer it is also as tyrannical as it is inevitable" (Green, 1986, p. 322).

The psychoanalyst's creative experience of writing is no different from the literary writer's. The analyst's anxieties and pleasures are the same as those of a poet, novelist, essayist, or playwright. As regards the creative process, the distance between penning a literary work and writing a psychoanalytic text is infinitely smaller than what the positivist scientist or the fictional writer may believe. In both forms of writing, great care is given to the aesthetic quality of language and to the precision with which concepts are expressed.

Having dealt with the similarities, we should now focus on crucial differences. For those who write literature, the written word is the paradigm of their expressivity. For analysts, by contrast, the text is not the ultimate goal. Even when written with great vehemence and conviction, its value is that of mediation between theory and clinical practice. Analysts are not renowned for their writing skills because there is something more significant for them than the text, and that is clinical work. Analytic dialogue provides the essential dimension of psychoanalytic identity.

The written and spoken words possess different values for writers and analysts. For writers, the spoken word plays a mediating role; for analysts, this role is assigned to writing. While the latter highly value the ability to explain theoretical, technical, or clinical reflections in writing, it is the spoken word that takes center stage in their work. The material they work with in psychoanalytic treatment is verbal. The spoken word is unpredictable. It can be neither erased nor deleted, and its value is irreplaceable.

Psychoanalysis, which is a comparatively young discipline, has turned the act of writing into a challenge whose stylistic specificity and complexity deserve consideration. Psychoanalytic theory is collectively constructed by way of writing. This process can only take place through the accumulation of individual contributions from different authors. The richness of the discipline stems from the diversity of these authors' styles, which provides complexity. When we sit down to write, the internal processing of multiple theories generates an energy that gives us the power to transform what we are writing. As a consequence, the theories that support our clinical practice lose their axiomatic quality and gradually reveal cracks and inconsistencies that had hitherto gone unnoticed.

The pen tends to give both shape and voice to thoughts that will remain unexplored if there is no attempt to capture them on paper. When analysts write, they seek to find congruence between the dialogue of the clinical experience and their theoretical references. In this way, they generate what André Green has called "the theoretical psychoanalytic process"

(Green, 1986, p. 16). Such congruence is relative – a meeting point of the vicissitudes of clinical practice and the concepts that support it. The partial divergence between clinical practice and theory can be stimulating and provides a fertile ground for the generation of new ideas.

The act of writing creates something new that was not present in the consulting room. Different threads of thought interweave outside the boundaries of the clinical experience and may be retrieved later within this setting. The ultimate goal of analytic writing is the analyst's constant transformation and the infusion of this newness into the analytic dialogue. By means of this dialogue, a new situation is created that was not present in the written text. This process involves a continuous back-and-forth between writing and clinical practice whereby the latter benefits from the creativeness of the former.

By writing a clinical paper, we aim to present and represent the experience shared by analyst and patient. In reality, writing adds a new dimension to that experience. Rather than a reproduction, it is a construction that becomes a new version. In truth, analytic writing "invents" a literary version of the clinical experience, an experience that can never be fully captured in words. We can compare writing with Freud's suggestion to Fliess in letter number 52: "the material present in the form of memory traces is being subjected from time to time to a *re-arrangement* in accordance with fresh circumstances – to a *re-transcription*" (Masson, 1985, p. 207; author's emphasis). To write is to produce a text that generates new and successive re-transcriptions.

Analysts' written work helps them question and challenge accepted theoretical beliefs. Inevitably, all theoretical psychoanalytic writing refers to clinical practice, which must be supported by theory. This cross-fertilization may result in the generation of new theories. There is a reciprocal relationship between these two dimensions, a feedback loop whereby each modifies the other. A constant dialectical process unfolds between dynamic clinical practice (and its theoretical foundation) and writing (and its clinical basis). Although not everything can be encapsulated in the written word, the writing process brings to light something new in the clinical dimension.

Chapter 12

Creating a link in the supervision space

Introduction

The title of this chapter emphasizes not only the need for a supervision space, but also the need to develop and construct, in this space, a creative and nurturing link between supervisor and supervisee. We believe that the following lines, written by Freud to Fliess, are highly significant: "I am curious to know whether you will confirm the diagnosis in the cases that I sent you," he tells him on May 30th, 1893 (Masson, 1985, p. 128). And in 1898 he writes, "I am so immensely glad that you are giving me the gift of the Other, a critic and reader – and one of your quality at that. I cannot write entirely without an audience, but do not at all mind writing only for you" (ibid., p. 313).

Every analyst needs a Wilhelm Fliess to correspond with. Maybe this exchange of letters contained the seed for what would become the supervision framework.[1] When Freud created the psychoanalytic device, some of his followers spontaneously began to discuss their patients with him. What prompted them to do that? What started the practice of supervision? It is hard to venture an answer. Supervision provides a space for the exploration of analysts' blind spots, their unconscious resistances, their ideologies, their ethics; it is a space for the comparison and reformulation of theories in relation to clinical practice.

It is also important to take into account that the need for supervision does not vanish just because institutional requirements have been fulfilled. Analysts typically request a supervision meeting when they have worries and concerns about their clinical practice and feel the need for guidance to overcome obstacles and make progress.

Yet something of the order of anxiety comes into play in the construction of the supervision space. While it offers continuity, the framework in which the process is inscribed does not provide any guarantees of quality or excellence. In this sense, supervision is a "legitimizing" space that does not ensure good practices.

Supervision: a space for transmission

Supervision provides a space for the transmission and understanding of psychoanalysis and its clinical practice. We are talking about transmission rather than just teaching or learning. Supervisors can learn to *facilitate* rather than *teach* (in the everyday sense of the word). Maud Mannoni (1989) claims that the supervision space is intended to develop in supervisees "an internal sensitivity to the analytic process." In addition, it produces effects that are key for the construction of analytic identity and satisfies an intrinsic need of analysts' professional life.

When transmission is successful, it generates a particular dynamic between supervisor and supervisee. Ideas flow in both directions. Following Bion's model, there is a two-way flow, a double-headed arrow that creates an "in-between" space. This space is connected with the link binding the two participants. We agree with Virginia Ungar when she emphasizes that the transmission process constitutes an emotional, transformative experience for both; changes taking place in the space of supervision are comparable to those occurring in the analytic process.

It is worth recalling here Freud's quote from Goethe's *Faust*: "What thou hast inherited from thy fathers, acquire it to make it thine" (Freud, 1912b, p. 158). Freud is challenging us by encouraging us to take his work and the work of his successors as a starting point for our own discoveries. We should not accept what has been said before without question. Transmission compels us to carry out our own personal exploration. This approach will enable us to incorporate existing ideas and build on them.

The private space of supervision facilitates the honing of the analytic function. This function is a product of the tolerance for psychic pain, of the capacity to listen and make decisions, which involves taking responsibility. It gives words value and effectiveness, thus creating the necessary conditions for working-through. However, this function may be lost, in which case we must work to restore it, or may be weakened to the point of disappearance.

In each individual's history, the developmental process of becoming an analyst is marked by the presence of a number of supervisors, which creates a multiple matrix. We believe that in every analyst's life history and career, the experience of working with different supervisions generates a space of great investiture and richness that promotes reflection on clinical practice.

The supervisor, a virtual third participant, operates in the analyst's mind as a symbolic mediator. At times, this virtual presence will have already modified the psychoanalytic field before a meeting between supervisor and supervisee actually takes place. On many occasions, the mere fact of requesting a supervision or preparing clinical material for review brings about changes in analysts' psyche that remove the obstacle that was hampering their work with the patient.

After a request for supervision, supervisees will often say to their supervisor, "When I called you, I really needed to talk to you urgently about a patient. But just after the call, I suddenly came up with a good idea, an insight, that could solve the problem." This insight will allow the analytic process to progress smoothly. We believe that the inclusion of a third party, the supervisor, makes it possible to examine the imaginary phantasmatic that may have enmeshed patient and analyst and upset the symbolic order. In this sense, we conceive of supervision as a framework that protects another framework.

Psychoanalytic institutions promote the development of complex networks due to cross-transferences of various kinds. Several types of bonds are simultaneously forged between patient and analyst, between analyst and supervisor, and between both analyst and supervisor and the institution. As Virginia Ungar (2011) states, "conflicts between analysts, teachers, supervisors and patients may inevitably reactivate in the supervisee's childlike experiences of insecurity, mistrust and conflicts" (Ungar, 2011,). This is the field where the dialectic between privacy and publicity and between uniqueness and diversity may be expressed.

Names

Naming is not an ingenuous act. To name something is to leave a mark in an attempt to draw boundaries. How can we interpret the name *supervision*? What does it reveal? In psychoanalytic institutions, we will hear different terms depending on the speaker's theoretical framework: *supervision*, *control analysis*, or *review*. These names are not random; they have been carefully chosen. We would like to examine them, along with some suggested variations.

> *Supervision*: This is the classical term that is most commonly used and most familiar to us. The word *supervision* can also be read as *super-vision*. In this sense, it alludes to the fact that analysts in training request supervision from analysts whose higher authority has been institutionally recognized and whose capacity for listening is deemed of great value. In doing so, analysts in training seek to legitimize their professional practice, sometimes in the belief that there is someone who has "super-knowledge" and can thus solve any clinical problem.
>
> *Control analysis*: This term is used by the French school of psychoanalysis. It can be conceived of as another analysis intended to work on those unanalyzed aspects of their psyche that are hampering analysts' clinical practice. It provides a space to help them deal with the anxiety triggered by their everyday work. The blind spots,

ideologies, ethical dilemmas, and challenges encountered in clinical practice that appear in the supervision space have led certain groups of analysts to argue that what happens in this space is closer to analysis than to the classical idea of supervision.

Re-view: Implicit in this word is the idea of revisiting or re-thinking clinical material to find something different or new. We can only reconstruct our train of thought, our interpretations, and other interventions after the fact, outside the psychoanalytic sessions. Whether in the context of a supervision or in a peer group, a review can produce an inter-vision.

Inter-vision: This term refers to an interconnection between patient, analyst, and supervisor based on the model of a complex network of thoughts. In such network, each person involved modifies and is modified by, and in, their interconnection. As we mentioned previously, there is a two-way flow that creates an "in-between" space. A fragment of the account of the session or the treatment interweaves with the associations of a second analyst. In this way, a new narrative may emerge that will produce unedited thoughts and feelings. In the "between analysts" space, ideas and conjectures are generated that open the possibility for acquiring a broader perspective. From our point of view, inter-vision is the ideal mode of functioning, and we try to take supervisions in this direction. What follows is an illustration of this process.

When Mary, a young analyst in training, started supervision, she was not seeing any patients at a high frequency of sessions. As a consequence, she was able to choose any of her patients for discussion in the supervision space. She was treating a very serious case that required frequent consultations. Sharon, a 17-year-old adolescent, was coming only once a week. She did not really want to be in analysis. She would repeatedly tell the analyst that she only came so that her parents, who had divorced four years earlier, would do her favors.

Sharon could not come on her own; she needed her mother to accompany her. She often arrived late or missed sessions because she overslept and her mother could not wake her up. Rather than resorting to interpretations, which Sharon would have found difficult to understand, the analyst tried to establish a link that would make it possible to "create" a patient so that interpretations could take place. Her major goal was to develop a genuine connection with her patient, which required actual communication. Only after almost a year did Sharon agree to a high frequency. Both supervisor and supervisee felt that every session with this patient might be the last one.

This material shows the work of supervision as a shared and evolving experience for both parties in the supervision couple and for the link that

112 Facing clinical challenges

binds them. As a team, supervisor and supervisee tackled the frustrations caused by the patient's refusal to establish a link, which was reflected in her frequent absences and late arrivals. As a result, the analyst was able to overcome her fear that the patient would leave and to feel confident that forging a link was actually possible.

Supervision provides a connection between theory, psychoanalytic technique, and clinical practice that enables the discovery of psychoanalytic phenomena and their meanings. In this way, it opens the possibility to develop a fresh perspective. This space is slightly less contaminated by the direct effects of the transference and countertransference. It is a third, alternative space where analysts may seek refuge from situations of paralyzing specularity. It thus contributes to strengthening symbolization and the transference, the two mainstays of the analytic process that ensure its continuity.

Supervision as a process

In their everyday professional and institutional life, analysts may encounter different settings where they can review clinical material. As we mentioned earlier, institutions offer a complex network of interconnections, a complexity stemming from the overlap of different types of transference that cover a broad spectrum. Furthermore, the position occupied by the institution both in the social imaginary and in each members' mind also plays a part.

Institutions have rules and ways of functioning that may limit the patient's choice of analyst and the analyst's choice of supervisor. Institutional guidelines regulate and condition professional practice. In addition, in this intersection of transferences and of different supervision settings resistances will appear. Different sorts of problems tend to emerge in these interstitial spaces.

In his fictional work *The Teachings of Don Juan*, Carlos Castaneda describes the challenges and obstacles we encounter in our search for knowledge. This author highlights the fear caused by learning something new, and warns that in order to learn, we must defy this fear. If we do, we will gradually reach "a clarity of mind which erases fear." This clarity, however, is actually an enemy, because besides dispelling fear, it blinds us; it makes us think that we can see clearly into everything. To fight this new enemy, says Don Juan, man "must do what he did with fear: he must defy clarity and use it only to *see*."

And once he is able to challenge clarity, he

> will arrive at a position where nothing can harm him anymore. . . . He will know at this point that the power he has been pursuing for so long is finally his. . . . His wish is the rule. He sees all that is around him. But he has also come across his third enemy: Power!
>
> (Castaneda, 1968, pp. 58–59)

As their professional identity develops, analysts must overcome similar obstacles. For this reason, the search for supervisors and the creation of spaces to revise clinical material are extremely important. Supervision is not just a mere supplement to our profession but one of its vital ingredients. Analysts' most private work is shared in a public forum devoted to the transmission of psychoanalysis, and is shared in such a way that the inscriptions of one generation can be passed down to another.

In addition to the plurality of methodological variants, we may distinguish three different moments in the supervision process: idealization, dis-idealization or disillusionment, and closure. These moments are not chronologically linear, and supervisees may experience more than one at a single meeting.

In 1991, when Silvia Resnizky was an analyst in training and part of the IPSO executive committee, she participated in a supervision study. The executive committee invited candidates from different regions of the world to take part in it. The study was published in an Argentine journal of one of our associations. The findings showed that in the supervision space, the openness to new ideas tends to coincide with the disruption of the supervisee's narcissistic equilibrium, a disruption that may be inherent in the nature of our relationship with knowledge.

When faced with new ways of thinking, supervisees may suddenly feel threatened and experience feelings of dis-identification. They are forced to confront their insecurities and fears. An initial tendency to attribute characteristics of the ego ideal to the supervisor is not uncommon. Supervisors are expected to know everything about the patient and about the identity of the analyst under supervision. This initial idealized transference sustains the work for some time. If the supervisor is assigned the role of the all-knowing expert, he or she will also occupy a position of power. Consequently, supervisors must keep this potential development in mind and work with their own narcissism to avoid encouraging idealization.

A more relaxed and comfortable atmosphere may be created if the supervisor helps the analyst overcome his or her insecurities. Uncertainties and multiple questions can then be voiced thanks to increased trust. Supervision becomes a space for inquiry. If this spirit of inquiry prevails, supervisor and supervisee can face together the obstacles and challenges arising from their review of clinical material. Dis-idealization and dis-identification processes will facilitate the creation of a new field where difficulties can be explored in greater depth and change can take place.

Disillusion and dis-idealization foster an attitude of discernment and, if the supervision process can tackle the questions that arise along with the associated frustrations, the continuity of the experience will not be affected. Yet if the idealization of the supervisee-supervisor link persists, the supervision process will be impoverished. Furthermore, the potential for discovery inherent in the analytic process may be reduced and even eliminated.

114 Facing clinical challenges

In this case, supervisees may become an echo of the supervisor and assimilate his or her ideas without the mediation of any personal working-through. As a result, they will be alienated from their own thoughts and will immerse themselves in the other's thinking, thus renouncing the autonomy of thought that analysts need to see themselves as creative and critical thinkers. Supervisors may play a part in this dynamic; it is not easy to give up the narcissistic benefit obtained and reinforced with the creation of small groups of faithful disciples.

In her book *Los destinos del placer* (*The Aims of Pleasure*) Piera Aulagnier (1980) mentions two different kinds of relationship between patient and analyst. One generates creativity and work, and the other involves mutual idealization. This description may fit the supervisor-supervisee dynamics. We can argue that both ways of relating involve modes of mental functioning that may coexist in the same link at different moments.

In addition, we can identify a stage of closure in the supervision process. What prevails in this stage is an atmosphere of demystification of super-visions and super-theories. In the above-mentioned study, the authors suggest that supervision be seen as a space for shared reflections on clinical practice. Certainties dissolve, and exchanging ideas promotes the development of a different, more flexible approach. Supervision, then, becomes an open door to a transformational space. Underlying this process is the desire to analyze and to be involved in the permanent rediscovery of the unconscious.

Becoming an analyst is an ongoing process; in each stage of the supervision, analysts' system of beliefs undergoes a slow transformation. As a result, new ideals and prejudices are formed in the search for a way of transforming obstacles into the driving force for the cure.

Self-management of supervision groups

Fraternal relationships reveal rivalries, tensions, conflicts that confront us with the "narcissism of small differences" (Freud, 1918). From the first biblical story of Cain and Abel, we have seen that the fraternal bond may become a condition for extreme rivalry and envy, and even arouse the desire to kill.

Then, what about the rivalry among analysts? We do not usually read or quote papers written by colleagues of our same generation. Zukerfeld and Zonis Zukerfeld (2013) carried out an interesting study that, among other topics, discussed our resistance to acknowledge our peers. Nevertheless, sharing and working with our peers can foster links based on hospitality that enable the establishment of fraternal bonds. Fraternity develops when we forge a fraternal link with a fellow human being. Yet for this to occur, the other must be perceived as a peer.

Self-managed supervision groups offer the possibility to build fraternal links. It is important to mention here that the IPA Working Parties, which are clinical discussion groups, have been both the framework and the inspiration for self-managed supervision groups. In these groups, the transference is not with the supervisor as a central figure but with the work of the supervision process itself. Free-flowing knowledge circulates among peers. This way of functioning allows different perspectives to coexist *without* the presence of a figure that acts as the provider of knowledge. Moreover, participants understand from the outset that there is no guarantee of a successful outcome.

Nonetheless, competition, rivalries, and power struggles also exist in these groups, as well as feelings of helplessness. If these difficulties can be overcome, instead of a super-vision, a dynamic of inter-vision will develop. In this context, an atmosphere of creativity and playfulness will afford the conditions for new discoveries to be made. In addition, group members' support and containment may result in the creation of social bonds.

The interaction among various ways of reflecting on the clinical material or on psychoanalytic theory triggers the creation of new meanings. This process, in turn, will have an impact on members' clinical work, as they will be able to consider each treatment from different perspectives. There is an interweaving of, or interconnection between, diverse approaches that complement or oppose one another.

What comes to light in this particular bond is the difference between diverse points of view. The contribution that each member makes denotes a specificity that brings into play what is usually referred to as a *style*. Like one's own name, this style results from the differentiation that arises as an effect of peer group work. Each individual's distinctive style can be recognized and valued.

These working groups show that the same clinical material may be read in different ways. Different interventions may thus be suggested that may be complementary but also incompatible. Contributions are influenced by both analysts' diverse theoretical frameworks and the specificity of their clinical practice, which, in turn, is marked by their professional and personal history. From 1983 on, Sandler's work focused on analysts' implicit, private, and preconscious theories, which underlie their clinical approach (Sandler, 1983). Group work is particularly effective in revealing these theories, which are often unknown to analysts themselves.

An example of a self-managed group

We would like to introduce a model that has been implemented in our association (Buenos Aires Psychoanalytic Association) over the last ten

years. There are several steady groups in operation with regular participants. They meet every two weeks, and have been running successfully
for many years.

While these groups are closed so as to foster a strong working dynamic
based on trust, a colleague from outside the group is invited to four-
session blocks. These sessions are held over a two-month period, and the
same clinical material is discussed in all of them. Guest members, who
may be members of other associations, play neither a coordinating nor a
supervising role, at least not in the traditional sense. Besides contributing
fresh ideas, they ensure through their presence a certain smoothness in
the group's dynamic. In this way, the tensions that inevitably appear in
a closed group, stemming from the tendency to develop fixed roles, are
reduced, as is the risk of stagnation.

After each block of four sessions, there are two meetings with no guests.
In this way, members can reflect on their previous discussions and review
both the theoretical-technical models used by the analyst who presented
the clinical material, and the models put forward by other participants.
The goal of this second phase is to identify the epistemological basis of our
clinical practice: what do we do, and why and how do we do it? We try
to detect the concepts and theoretical frameworks implicit in the analyst's
interventions and in group members' contributions.

This experience has proved to be very successful. That is why we
believe it is important to foster the creation of clinical workshops with
peer groups in our institutions as an essential part of our ongoing professional development.

To conclude

The supervision framework and process provide a setting that is con-
ducive to the transmission and understanding of psychoanalysis and its
practice insofar as it builds a bridge between the public and private settings. Clinical practice does not fit perfectly into psychoanalytic theory.
There are no theories that can fully explain what happens in clinical work,
because this work involves constant change and rebuilding. This struc-
tural discrepancy generates an anxiety that constantly oscillates between
knowledge and ignorance, which are separated by an unbridgeable gap.

Perhaps the true demand for supervision derives from the solitary
nature of analytic practice and from the obstacles that may be associated
with this condition – isolation, narcissistic withdrawal, specularity. It
can be argued that supervision emerges from the psychoanalytic device.
Seen from this perspective, supervision is not inside or outside but "in
between" the psychoanalytic process.

It is vital that we give further consideration to clinical practice. This aspect
of psychoanalysis needs and demands its own space of resignification,

with the presence of an other who serves as a mediating participant. In our experience, ongoing participation in a clinical working group fosters strong links and a spirit of solidarity among group members.

Note

1 According to Freud, Fliess was an attentive and often enthusiastic listener. Their friendship (1858–1928), the closest one we know of in Freud's life, was strongly tied to his work and was both stimulating and constraining.

Chapter 13

Between analysts

"If anyone speaks, it gets light."

Sigmund Freud (1905)

This chapter reflects on the relationships analysts forge among ourselves. We delve into the psychoanalytic profession by analyzing institutional life – the value of membership and the peer bonds that develop in institutions. In addition, we discuss the experience of two groups of analysts, focusing on the unique dynamics of their encounters.

In her tribute to Grace Frick, M. Yourcenar writes that

> there must have been sometimes, in the background, perhaps . . . someone who bolsters our courage and approves, or sometimes disputes, our ideas; who shares with us, and with equal fervor . . . someone who is neither our shadow nor our reflection, nor even our complement, but simply himself; someone who leaves us ideally free, but who nevertheless obliges us to be fully what we are.
>
> (Yourcenar, 1974, p. 343)

We start from the idea that the peer dimension facilitates modes of production that enhance thinking, creativity, and the many variants of membership. By supplementing institutional training, these horizontal links among colleagues provide a working environment whose effects also influence clinical work.

Links among peers are the condition of possibility for social bonding. Peers support each other by being legitimate interlocutors. They take on their ethical responsibility, which involves caring and respecting the other as a fellow being, alien and different, as well as preserving the habitat and dwelling we share with other living beings. We believe that in this second century of life of psychoanalysis we need to create new work spaces and new ways of working with each other. Moreover, sharing experiences with colleagues contributes to sustaining our access to the unconscious.

The traditional psychoanalytic view of family links, based on parent-child differentiation, gradually made room for other distinctions. The presence of the other as *fellow being* and, at the same time, as *alien-different* generates new ways of coming together (*hermanarse*)[1] to interact. Such presence is tied to René Kaës's (2004) concept of mutual anaclisis, which refers to reciprocal support among subjects. We simultaneously seek support from and support others.

Fraternal bonds challenge the myth, founded on solipsistic conceptualizations, that downplays the role of the fraternal dimension in the family and social settings. Besides having become an object of research, fraternity also constitutes a practice and a way of life. For this reason, we need to analyze critically the social and subjective status of phratries. The goal is to reassess potential linking strategies from the perspective of an ethics of responsibility, which, far from suffocating uniqueness, supplements it and increases its complexity.

One of the downsides of globalization is that it tends to dissolve difference into a suffocating homogeneity. A fruitful globalization under moderately democratic conditions should operate as a platform to promote the recognition of difference. It should be based on an ethics of *doing along with others*, that is, on an intersubjective configuration that intertwines with desire. This ethics develops in the immanence of links, in their ongoing flow.

At the same time, fraternal relationships reveal rivalries, tensions, conflicts that confront us with the "narcissism of small differences" (Freud, 1918). We've known since the first biblical story that the fraternal bond may become the site of a wild display of rivalry, envy, and even annihilating power. As we have mentioned earlier,[2] R. Zukerfeld and R. Zonis Zukerfeld carried out an insightful research that shows our resistance to acknowledging our peers.

Fraternal collectives

Practicing parity, that is, working in a horizontal manner with mutual respect and reciprocity entails the existence of a group production that circulates as its cultural legacy (Magris, 2001). Leadership among peers may be a paradoxical notion, but there is usually an individual who takes on the responsibility of coordinating groups, a traditional figure in medieval culture who is primus inter pares,[3] the first among equals, despite being a peer. He or she is the most experienced in certain issues, and this type of leadership is generally rotating and operational. The peers themselves elect a successor following a self-management procedure.

In the specific field of psychoanalysis, peers create a mode of operation whose goal is to establish symmetrical relations where difference is generated without relying on a figure of established knowledge. Sharing concerns and interests creates an interplay among peers that helps hone our analytic tools. The range of potential ways to address conflict and suffering and the multiple perspectives offered by this peer link show the inevitable disparity of viewpoints. What each person proposes to the group requires the intervention of the others. To practice parity, we must assign our peers a leading role as favored interlocutors.

Over time, continuous peer work will lead to the development of a style. Like a name, a style is the distinction that may arise as a possible effect of production in a professional group. It is a new way of showing the existence of diversity and uniqueness in peer relationships; it is both a link and a personal creation. Each name acquires singularity by way of the blending of individual features with the particular "effect of meeting" brought about by the interaction among group members, an effect that becomes evident both in the process and in the final outcome.

The same movement with which we open a space contributes to the creation of individual identities, and this creation, in turn, will affect the entire history of the group. Thus, we bring into play the alienness in ourselves and the sameness of the alien. Diversity occurs within the group as a result of the presence of the other. This is the "effect of presence" of inhabiting a situation, of being with others.

Focusing on the fraternal dimension raises the question of the fellow being in its three registers, namely, imaginary, symbolic, and real. The dialogue among analysts entails assigning a very important role to listening, to the ability to tolerate conjecture, and to feeling one's way. The phrase *between analysts* implies a particular form of dialogue in which all certainty is removed. The *between* occurs when conjecture predominates. The *between* is a figure that is neither I nor the other, but rather what is produced in the encounter between the two.

The encounter between analysts implies the possibility of disagreement. Our availability to belong to these groups supplements professional life from a different vantage point. Sharing experiences, questions, uncertainties is a worthwhile endeavor. Quoting Chesterton, J.-B. Pontalis calls the link *between* analysts "the Club of Queer Trades." This author remarks on the strangeness of analytic work, and expresses the wish that "our psychoanalytic societies were clubs where getting together were a pleasure for decent people who could ask each other questions" (Pontalis, 2007, p. 54). The irony in Pontalis's statement reveals how unusual and difficult it is to fulfill this wish. However, the work these groups structured around horizontal links must perform is aimed to legitimize their production.

These groups ought to offer a space to think aloud and discuss ideas that are not fully fleshed out. There, a convergence, an alchemy would be produced between the intimacy of clinical practice and the exposure to the

Between analysts   121

public from which a creative process might arise that goes against formality and bureaucracy. For such alchemy to develop, we must be willing to reveal our hesitant thoughts without resorting to previously established knowledge. Paradoxically, we rely on our peers both to assert ourselves and to think independently.

Our institutions

Our unique path toward becoming analysts is marked not only by analyses, supervisions, mentors, and readings, but also by a sense of institutional belonging and our sharing experiences with peer colleagues. Fraternal links established during our training and in scientific meetings and conferences remain an important part of our scientific and social network. Furthermore, a transference involving a certain degree of idealization is integral to the choice of institutional affiliation.

Membership awakes the illusion of homogeneity. Differences can enrich us, but may also be difficult to tolerate and may eventually become a source of conflict. The violent irruption of heterogeneity can be viewed as negative. Some groups are better than others at tolerating the alternation between creativity and stagnation. Bureaucratization can cause discomfort and feelings of helplessness, emptiness, and anger. Enriquez (1989) writes about resistance to change as a defense against lack of structure, the drives, our fellow beings, and the unknown.

What resources do we have to support our work as analysts? One of them is writing and group production. There are also other instances of belonging, such as spaces where we can share our clinical experience and active participation in the different areas of institutional life. As we pointed out in the previous chapter, the networks that develop in psychoanalytic institutions are complex due to the crossing of transferences of various kinds. This is the field where the dialectic between privacy and exposure, between uniqueness and diversity can be expressed. "Holding the unconscious open is not an easy task," states Paz, "and ultimately, the fruitfulness of institutional membership is measured by its contribution to maintaining a sense of belonging in various ways" (Paz, 2008, p. 69).

Institutional devices such as clinical meetings, seminars, supervisions, symposia, workshops, and conferences also provide support. We interact in formal institutional frameworks as well as in informal frameworks outside institutions – in their margins and hallways. We simultaneously inhabit different spaces of belonging, and diverse ways of belonging coexist. Listening and creativity are encouraged in certain contexts and times and thwarted in others. Our institutions should maintain an ongoing dialogue with other disciplines and, at the same time, be alert to the shifting configurations of social bonds.

122 Facing clinical challenges

Levinas (1986) evokes two metaphors that refer to two different ways of producing thought. The Greeks created the metaphor of Ulysses, the hero of a thousand battles who, after wandering for years, returns home to Ithaca. In contrast, the Jewish metaphor of Abraham alludes to those who leave home never to return. In Levinas's words,

> A work conceived radically is a movement of the same unto the other which never returns to the same. To the myth of Ulysses returning to Ithaca, we wish to oppose the story of Abraham who leaves his fatherland forever for a yet unknown land, and forbids his servant to even bring back his son to the point of departure.
>
> (Levinas, 1986, p. 340)

These two figures point to two methods of production within a link. The first one produces knowledge by confirming identity regardless of the other; I am like this, and I have always been like this. The other one rests on difference. It confirms that identity entails difference – that by being with others, we are no longer the same.

What leads us to devote ourselves to psychoanalysis? What kind of calling is this? Why do we rarely talk about the childhood sources of our psychoanalytic calling? Pontalis writes that while Freud was not fond of confessions, he revealed more about himself than any of us does. Perhaps, sheltered by neutrality and abstinence, we leave ourselves in the margins.

These and other concerns led us to include the voices of other analysts in an earlier book (Mauer, Moscona, and Resnizky, 2002). To do so, we met with Etchegoyen, Puget, Berenstein, Levin, Garma, and Hornstein and gathered their testimonies. In one of these conversations Levin traces the possible origin of the psychoanalytic calling back to childhood, where an ethical position can be identified that recognizes and validates unconscious formations. This position involves acknowledging and prioritizing the unconscious from the beginning

Pontalis (2007) quotes the novel *The Dark Journey*, by Julien Green, where one of the characters is portrayed as driven by passion and having a curiosity whose goal is not to know but to live in the neighborhood of the unknown. This character aspires to guess not the secret but the presence of the secret. According to Pontalis, such a description may very well serve to account for the desire to become and remain an analyst. As Freud put it,

> I am actually not at all a man of science, not an observer, not an experimenter, not a thinker. I am by temperament nothing but an adventurer with all the curiosity, daring and tenacity characteristic of a man of this sort.
>
> (Masson, 1985, p. 398)

Parity and fraternity

The concepts of parity and fraternity are often used interchangeably. In fact, they can be read as synonyms with regard to the notion of kinship; siblings are kin. Nonetheless, there are differences between the two. Parity implies a longing for homogenization, for integration into a totality. Sameness prevails over difference. Parity results from belonging to a generic group. In our case, we are middle-class Argentineans living in the same neighborhood. Fraternity, by contrast, includes a more intense and, simultaneously, disturbing dimension of intimacy.

We can recognize ourselves in our siblings because we share an origin. Yet, at the same time, we cannot recognize ourselves in them because their differences deny our narcissistic desire for homogeneity. Fraternity involves both an endless yearning for differentiation and an irreducible desire for uniformity. It is a question of withstanding this paradox, a permanent and irresolvable tension.

Fraternity is a construction in the sense that you adopt a sibling – you create a fraternal link with a fellow being. Nonetheless, such construction is impossible without the acknowledgment of a parity.

An autobiographical experience

It is a peculiar feature of our impossible profession that our own unconscious and our psychoanalytic ways of thinking are both a working tool and an object of study. Over two decades ago, the three authors of this book started our Saturday working breakfasts. We met at a cafe for a couple of hours, without the pressure or troubles of working days. This group started as a production space, a writing space. Our sole aim was to present individual papers at conferences or symposia.

Writing became its leitmotif as well as its greatest challenge. For us, writing is a method of study; it is a way of thinking about the issues that interest us and, of course, about the issues that concern us. It is curious and significant that from the outset, the thread that connected the subjects that called our attention was the analyst's viewpoint. Our first book, published in 2002, was the outcome of that journey.

For five or six years of intense group work, we traveled on inhospitable, seldom-visited paths, such as ethics in psychoanalysis, analysts' dreams, their writing and ideology, their anxieties, their belongings. Bar Abierto, a cafe on Serrano Square, was the setting for the first stage of our joint work. It was an era of rough drafts, manuscripts, and almost illegible photocopies with plenty of handwritten amendments. "Cut and paste" was a literal act performed with scissors and glue.

No one missed a meeting. It was not uncommon to get there after a sleepless night and be unable to offer ideas or insights. Still, our commitment

124   Facing clinical challenges

and reliability sustained the will and pleasure of meeting without fail, of preserving our space. Over time, we developed a deep affection for our writing quest. Our Saturday mornings were non-negotiable. This fraternal group of peers, friends, and colleagues offered a comfortable space where to think freely. Willing to take on the challenge of wandering without direction, we became excited about different topics, sometimes predominantly clinical, and other times more theoretical and technical.

Obviously, our trio has not survived by withdrawing into itself. Its interdependence has manifold facets. First, our membership in the Buenos Aires Psychoanalytic Society is an inscription that sustains us. This is our institution; we keep growing year after year thanks to its symposia, its publications, and our interactions with our teachers. Second, our group has found an excellent interlocutor in a contemporary thinker, as well as philosopher and writer, who is, above all, a friend who listens to, decodes, corrects, and guides us. Santiago Kovadloff, with whom we have worked regularly from the beginning, vitally nurtures our efforts and our pleasure in our ongoing work.

We have worked in so many different ways that we could not even attempt to describe them. At first, we wrote and revised together until the text became the expression of just one voice. Back then, the personal computer was not part of the creative process but offered its own contribution when the writing was completed. Printed letters dressed the manuscript; they made it presentable.

Later, the ability to make amendments via electronic devices modified our methodology. We started writing separately, and every draft went through multiple versions that each of us successively modified. At this point, the group dynamics somewhat changed without replacing the original arrangement.

Our own style started to develop in the framework of this experience of meeting in an environment of trust, empathy, and availability to think. The fact that differences within the group are expressed and supported is almost a truism. At the same time, the fact that the group oscillates and is disparate yet a source of support for every one of us is not so obvious. Undoubtedly, we complement each other in some cases, we serve as a supplement in others, and we tolerate our uneven contributions in still others.

Various reasons, such as institutional commitments and personal or family troubles, temporarily affected our availability to write. Nonetheless, the group think tank was always preserved as a shared space. We started a workshop to incorporate new authors and other standpoints, revisited old themes, and delved into neighboring fields such as philosophy or literature. During the last decade, we also made a nest in other coffee shops such as Persicco, where countless coffees accompanied our meetings. We got there every Saturday at 9 AM to discuss ideas and share anxieties, professional misfortunes, and joint projects. For many years, Vicente Galli was a warm and encouraging witness to our group's perseverance.

Technology helped us work together. It allowed us to share files and texts that were simultaneously modified and polished. Great inventions such as Dropbox store and support the endless dalliances and erasures that occur between the rough draft and the publication of a paper. However, marvelous technological inventions can shock their users when awkwardly handled, as has unquestionably happened to us. The risk of stumbling upon a warning that confirms that the book has been completely deleted by one of us can cloud the happiest moment!

Joint writing is also a complex device that becomes laborious, intensive, and stressful at times as publication approaches. Many hours of editing, the need to expand concepts, authors, and quotes, and the tension between our eagerness to see the book ready and our resistance to let it go, all play a role in the final stretch. Group work, in turn, generates more interaction between collective production and the backstage of our individual consulting rooms.

The clinical cases that illustrate the chapters of this book stem from the interaction among our separate clinical practices. The ample availability demanded by this shared adventure render it both interesting and difficult to communicate. Investing in such a committed joint project involves agreeing not only on ideas, but also on the selection of clinical materials and the publishing contract. It requires giving up authors, assigning tasks, and trusting. Our writing, which has become more particular over the years, permanently requires that we strike a balance between insisting on our own ideas and pleasing the others. Sometimes we have to consent to deleting entire paragraphs.

In a peer group there is room for hesitation and dissent as well as for delight in the face of achievement. The network creates cohesion and trains us in open-mindedness, responsibility, and solidarity. It is a way of life in which thinking is associated with the adventure of not knowing where we are headed.

On the dynamics of a meeting among professionals

Different accounts of the Psychological Wednesday Society, or Wednesday Group, tell us that five colleagues met once a week to exchange ideas about a paper. Topics ranged from clinical cases to the application of psychoanalysis to literary works, and the papers presented could be previews of future publications. The first one discussed the effects of tobacco (Nunberg and Federn, 1962). Stekel found the early meetings inspiring; Graf recalls their ritual-like nature. First, one of the members would read an entire paper without being interrupted. Then they had coffee and pastries, and the discussion began after a quarter of an hour of pleasantries (Gay, 1988).

It is worth adding some further detail about this group of analysts – about its origin, context, and work. It all started at Freud's home in Vienna in the fall of 1902. Steckel, Adler, Reitler, and Kahane would gather there every Wednesday evening. Soon after, Graff, Rank, Jung, Abraham, Jones, and Ferenczi joined them. Some years later, in 1908, the Vienna Psychoanalytic Society developed from that informal group, which Freud had called *the gang* when introducing it to Ludwig Binswanger.

The dissolution of the Wednesday Society marks the beginning of institutionalization. While organization and the increased potential for the dissemination of ideas represent a gain, spontaneity is lost. Institutions are endowed with a system to interpret the Fundamental Law. The advantage of peer work is that it promotes the development of a hospitality link. Derrida (2000) argues that hospitality belongs neither to the host nor to the guest; the hospitable act inscribes giver and receiver simultaneously.

Notes

1 See note 5 in Chapter 7.
2 See Chapter 12.
3 The feudal lords chose a primus inter pares as the one who should become king. This lord was just another member of the group; he was not above the others, nor was his position granted through inheritance.

Bibliography

Agamben, G. (1978). *Infancy and History: Essays on the Destruction of Experience.* Translated by Liz Heron. London: Verso, 1993.

Agamben, G. (2009). *What Is an Apparatus and Other Essays.* Translated by David Kishik and Stefan Pedatella. Stanford, CA: Stanford University Press.

Assoun, P.-L. (2000). *Lecciones psicoanalíticas sobre hermanos y hermanas* [Psychoanalytic Lessons on Siblings]. Buenos Aires: Nueva Visión.

Assoun, P.-L. (2004). *Corps et symptôme* [Body and Symptom]. Paris: Anthropos.

Aulagnier, P. (1980). *Los destinos del placer* [The Aims of Pleasure]. Barcelona: Petrel.

Aulagnier, P. (1984). *El aprendiz de historiador y el maestro brujo: Del discurso identificante al discurso delirante* [The Apprentice Historian and the Master Sorcerer: From Identifying Discourse to Delirious Discourse]. Translated by José Luis Etcheverry. Buenos Aires: Amorrortu.

Aulagnier, P. (1989). *Trastornos psicóticos de la personalidad o psicosis* [Psychotic Personality Disorders or Psychosis]. Presented at the 36th IPA Congress, Rome, July.

Aulagnier, P. (1991). Construirse un pasado [Creating a past for oneself]. *Revista de psicoanálisis*, 13 (3): 441–468.

Ayuso Díez, J. M. (1985). Introducción [Introduction]. In: E. Levinas, ed., *Ética e infinito* [Ethics and Infinity], op. cit.

Badiou, A. (2005). *Being and Event.* Translated by Oliver Feltham. New York: Continuum.

Ball, A. L. (2014). Hombre, mujer ... intersexo: qué sos en Facebook? [Man, Woman, or ... Intersex: What Are you on Facebook?]. *La Nación*, April 12.

Baranger, W. (1991). Narcissism in Freud. In: *Freud's "On Narcissism": An Introduction.* Edited by J. Sandler, P. Fonagy, and E. S. Person. New Haven: Yale University Press for The International Psychoanalytical Association, pp. 108–130 [El narcicismo en Freud. In: J. Sandler, ed., *Estudio sobre "Introducción al narcisismo" de Sigmund Freud.* Madrid: Julián Yebenes, pp. 127–151].

Baranger, M. and Baranger, W. (1961–1962). La situación analítica como campo dinámico. *Revista uruguaya de Psicoanálisis*, IV (1): 3–54.

Baranger, M., Baranger, W. and Mom, J. M. (1983). Process and non-process in analytic work. *The International Journal of Psychoanalysis*, 64: 1–15.

Baranger, W., Baranger, M. and Mom, J. M. (1988). The infantile psychic trauma from us to Freud: Pure trauma, retroactivity and reconstruction. *The International Journal of Psychoanalysis*, 69: 113–128 [Baranger, M, Baranger, W., Mom, J. (1987).

Bibliography

El trauma psíquico infantil, de nosotros a Freud. *Revista de la Asociación Psicoanalítica Argentina*, XLIV (4)].

Berenstein, I. (2001). *El sujeto y el otro: De la ausencia a la presencia* [The Subject and the Other: From Absence to Presence]. Buenos Aires: Paidós.

Berenstein, I. (2004a). *Devenir otro con otro(s)* [Becoming Other with Other(s)]. Buenos Aires: Paidós.

Berenstein, I. (2004b). El sujeto como otro entre (inter) otros [The Subject as other between (inter) others]. In: *El otro en la trama intersubjetiva* [The Other in the Intersubjective Web]. Edited by L. Glocer Fiorini. Buenos Aires: Lugar, pp. 75–97.

Berflein, E. et al. (2003). *Entre hermanos: Sentido y efectos del vínculo fraterno* [Among Siblings: Meaning and Effects of the Fraternal Link]. Buenos Aires: Lugar.

Bianchi, G. (2005). *Sufrimiento en los vínculos* [Suffering in Links]. Presented at the International Psychotherapy Conference, Buenos Aires, July.

Bion, W. R. (1962). *Learning from Experience*. London: Heinemann.

Blanchot, M. (1980). *The Writing of the Disaster*. Translated by Ann Smock. Lincoln: University of Nebraska Press, 1986.

Bleger, J. (1967). *Symbiosis and Ambiguity: A Psychoanalytic Study*. Edited by John Churcher and Leopoldo Bleger. Translated by John Churcher, Leopoldo Bleger, and Susan Rogers. East Sussex and New York: Routledge, 2013.

Bleichmar, S. (2005). *La subjetividad en riesgo* [Subjectivity at Risk]. Buenos Aires: Topia.

Bleichmar, S. (2009). Prólogo [Prologue]. In: *Paradojas de la sexualidad masculina* [Paradoxes of Male Sexuality]. Buenos Aires: Paidós, pp. 9–12.

Bleichmar, S. (2010). Las nuevas cuestiones ponen en crisis viejas teorías [New Issues Lead to the Crisis of Old Theories]. Interview with E. Rotenberg. In: *Homoparentalidades: Nuevas familias* [Same-Sex Parenting, New Families]. Edited by E. Rotenberg and B. Agrest Wainer. Buenos Aires: Lugar, pp. 91–98.

Borges, J. L. et. al. (1984). *Del escrito* [On Writing]. Buenos Aires: Letra Viva.

Castaneda, C. (1968). *The Teachings of Don Juan: A Yaqui Way of Knowledge*. Berkeley: University of California Press [*Las enseñanzas de Don Juan*. México: FCE, 1974].

Castro, E. (2004). *El vocabulario de Michel Foucault: Un recorrido alfabético por sus temas, conceptos y autores* [Michel Foucault's Vocabulary: An Alphabetical Journey through Topics, Concepts, and Authors]. Quilmes: Universidad Nacional de Quilmes.

Castro, E. (2011). *Diccionario Foucault* [Foucault Dictionary]. Buenos Aires: Siglo XXI.

Castro Orellana, R. (2008). *Ética para un rostro de arena: Michel Foucault y el cuidado de la libertad* [Ethics for a Face of Sand: Michel Foucault and the Care for Freedom]. Chile: LOM.

Casullo, A. and Resnizky, S. (1993). Supervisión psicoanalítica: enfoque clínico o reflexiones clínicas compartidas [Psychoanalytic supervision: Clinical Approach or Shared Clinical Reflections]. *Revista de Psicoanálisis*, 1 (4/5): 1043–1052.

Dalí, S. (1976). *The Unspeakable Confessions of Salvador Dali, as Told to André Parinaud*. Translated by Harold J. Salemson. London: W. H. Allen.

De Cristoforis, O. (2009). *Amores y parejas en el siglo XXI* [Love and Couples in the Twenty-First Century]. Buenos Aires: Letra Viva.

Deleuze, G. (2006). What is a *dispositif?* In: *Two Regimes of Madness: Texts and Interviews 1975–1995*. Edited by David Lapoujade. Translated by Ames Hodges and Mike Taormina. Los Angeles and New York: Semiotext(e), pp. 343–352.

Bibliography 129

Derrida, J. (1978). *Writing and Difference*. Translated by Alan Bass. London: Routledge and Kegan Paul.

Derrida, J. (2000). *Of Hospitality: Anne Dufourmantelle Invites Jacques Derrida to Respond*. Translated by Rachel Bowlby. Stanford, CA: Stanford University Press [*Anne Dufourmantelle invite Jacques Derrida a répondre De l'hospitalité*. Paris: Calman-Levy, 1997].

Droeven, J., ed. (2002). *Sangre o elección, construcción fraterna* [Blood or Choice, Fraternal Construction]. Buenos Aires: del Zorzal.

Enriquez, E. (1989). El trabajo de la muerte en las instituciones [The work of death in institutions]. In: *La institución y las instituciones* [The Institution and Institutions]. Edited by R. Kaës. Buenos Aires: Paidós, pp. 89–92.

Etchegoyen, H. (1986). *Fundamentals of Psychoanalytic Technique*, revised edition. London: Karnac, 1999.

Fernández, A. M. (2007). *Las lógicas colectivas. Imaginarios, cuerpos y multiplicidades* [Collective Logics: Imaginaries, Bodies, and Multiplicities]. Buenos Aires: Biblos.

Fernández, A. M. (2012). *Las lógicas sexuales: amor, política y violencias* [Sexual Logics: Love, Politics and Forms of Violence]. Buenos Aires: Nueva Visión.

Fernández, A. M., Borakievich, S., Cabrera, C. and Ortiz Molinuevo, S. (2014). La indagación de las implicaciones y el pensar-en-situación: una contribución de la metodología de problematización recursiva [Inquiring into implications and in-situation-thinking: A contribution of recursive problematization methodology]. *Revista Sujeto, Subjetividad y Cultura*, 8: 21–28.

Foucault, M. (1976–1988). Structuralisme et poststructuralisme. In *Dits et écrits*. Paris: Gallimard. Vol. II, p. 1267.

Foucault, M. (1978). *The History of Sexuality: An Introduction*. Vol. I. Translated by Robert Hurley. New York: Random House, 1978.

Foucault, M. (1994). Structuralism and post-structuralism. In *Aesthetics, Method, and Epistemology. Essential Works of Foucault, 1954–1984*. Vol. II. Edited by James D. Faubion. Translated by Robert Hurley and others. New York: The New Press, 1998, pp. 433–458.

Foucault, M. (2003). *"Society Must Be Defended": Lectures at the Collège de France, 1975–1976*. Edited by Mauro Berani and Alessandro Fontana. Translated by David Macey. New York: Picador.

Freud, S. (1895). Project for a scientific psychology. *S. E.*, 1: 281–391 [*Proyecto de psicología*. T. I. O. C. Buenos Aires: Amorrortu, 1950].

Freud, S. (1899). Screen memories. *S. E.*, 3: 301–322 [Sobre los recuerdos encubridores. T. III. O. C. Buenos Aires and Madrid: Amorrortu, 1981].

Freud, S. (1905). Three essays on the theory of sexuality. *S. E.*, 7: 125–248.

Freud, S. (1912a). Recommendations to physicians practising psycho-analysis. *S. E.*, 12: 109–120.

Freud, S. (1912b). *Totem and taboo. S. E.*, 13: ix–164.

Freud, S. (1914). Remembering, repeating and working-through. *S. E.*, 12: 145–157. [Recordar, repetir, reelaborar. T. XII. O. C. Buenos Aires: Amorrortu, 1980].

Freud, S. (1916). Introductory lectures on psycho-analysis. *S. E.*, 15: 1–240.

Freud, S. (1918). The taboo of virginity. *S. E.*, 11: 191–208.

Freud, S. (1919). The uncanny. *S.E.*, 17: 219–256. [Lo ominoso. T. XVII. O. C. Buenos Aires: Amorrortu].

130 Bibliography

Freud, S. (1921). Group psychology and the analysis of the ego. *S. E.*, 18: 67–145 [*Psicología de las masas y análisis del yo*, T. XVIII. O. C. Buenos Aires: Amorrortu].

Freud, S. (1922). Some neurotic mechanisms in jealousy, paranoia and homosexuality. *S. E.*, 18: 221–233.

Freud, S. (1925). A note upon the "mystic writing pad." *S. E.*, 19: 227–234.

Freud, S. (1926). Inhibitions, symptoms and anxiety. *S. E.*, 20: 77–178 [Inhibición, síntoma y angustia. T. XX. O. C. Buenos Aires: Amorrortu].

Freud, S. (1930). *Civilization and its Discontents. S. E.*, 21: 59–148 [*El malestar en la cultura*, T. XXI, O. C. Buenos Aires: Amorrortu].

Freud, S. (1933). The dissection of the psychical personality. In: *New Introductory Lectures on Psychoanalysis, S. E.*, 22: 57–80.

Freud, S. (1939). *Moses and Monotheism. S. E.*, 23: 3–140. [*Moisés y el monoteísmo*, T. XXIII. O. C. Buenos Aires: Amorrortu].

Freud, S. (1950 [1895]). Project for a scientific psychology. *S. E.*, 1: 281–391 [*Proyecto de psicología*. T. I. O. C. Buenos Aires: Amorrortu].

Freud, S. (1970). *Letters of Sigmund Freud, 1873–1939*. Translated by Tania Stern and James Stern. London: Hogarth.

Gaspari, R. (2003). Cuando los padres son un imposible [When parents constitute an impossible]. In: E. Berflein et al., eds., *Entre Hermanos: Sentidos y efectos del vínculo fraterno*, op. cit., pp. 301–306.

Gay, P. (1988). *Freud: A Life of Our Time*. New York and London: W. W. Norton.

Glocer Fiorini, L. (2010). Presentaciones cambiantes de la sexualidad [Changing presentations of sexuality]. *Revista Uruguaya de Psicoanálisis*, 111: 44–53.

Gomel, S. (1976). *Transmisión generacional, familia y subjetividad* [Generational Transmission, Family, and Subjectivity]. Buenos Aires: Lugar, 1997.

Gomel, S. and Matus, S. (2011). *Conjeturas psicopatológicas* [Psychopathological Conjectures]. Buenos Aires: Psicolibro.

Green, A. (1986). *On Private Madness*. Madison, CT: International Universities Press [*De locuras privadas*. Buenos Aires: Amorrortu, 1990].

Han, B-C. (2015). *The Burnout Society*. Translated by Erik Butler. Redwood City, CA: Standford University Press [*La sociedad del cansancio*. Barcelona: Herder, 2012].

Jelin, E. (2002). *State Repression and the Labors of Memory*. Translated by Judy Rein and Marcial Godoy Anativia. Minneapolis: University of Minnesotta Press, 2003.

Juarroz, R. (1991). Creación poética [Poetic creation]. In: *La creación del arte. Incidencias freudianas* [Art Creation: Freudian Influences]. Edited by I. Vegh. Buenos Aires: Nueva Visión.

Jullien, F. (2013). *Cinco conceptos propuestos al psicoanálisis* [Five Concepts Suggested to Psychoanalysis]. Buenos Aires: El Cuenco de Plata.

Kaës, R. (1991). El pacto denegativo en los conjuntos tran-subjetivos [The denial pact in transubjective groups]. In: *Lo negativo: figuras y modalidades* [The Negative: Figures and Modalities]. Edited by A. Missenard et al. Buenos Aires: Amorrortu, pp. 130–170.

Kaës, R. (1999). *Las teorías psicoanalíticas del grupo*. Buenos Aires: Amorrortu. [A hypothesis for a third topic regarding intersubjectivity and the subject in a common, shared psychic space. Translated by Deberah Cats. *Funzione Gamma*. No. 426, 2004, no pagination. Available at www.funzionegamma.it/wp-content/uploads/hypothesis-topic.pdf].

Kaës, R. (2006). *Linking, Alliances, and Shared Space: Groups and the Psychoanalyst*. Translated by Andrew Weller. London: Karnac Books. The International Psychoanalysis Library Series.

Kancyper, L. (2003). *Jorge Luis Borges o la pasión de la amistad* [Jorge Luis Borges or, The Passion for Friendship]. Buenos Aires: Lumen.

Kancyper, L. (2004). *El complejo fraterno. Estudio psicoanalítico* [The Fraternal Complex: A Psychoanalytic Study]. Buenos Aires: Lumen.

Kovadloff, S. (1993). *El silencio primordial* [Primordial Silence]. Buenos Aires: Emecé.

Kovadloff, S. (2008). *El enigma del sufrimiento* [The Enigma of Suffering]. Buenos Aires: Emecé.

Kovadloff, S. y Tesone, J. E. (2002). "Cuando la psiquiatría se aleja del hombre" [When psychiatry distances itself from human beings]. *La Nación Daily*, October 1.

Krakov, H. (1988). Resistencias a la vincularidad [Resistances to linking]. In: *Diccionario de las configuraciones vinculares* [Dictionary of Link Configurations]. Edited by C. Pachuk and R. Friedler. Buenos Aires: del Candil, pp. 395–400.

Kuras de Mauer, S. and May, N. (2001). El trabajo de parentalidad [The work of parenting]. *Revista de la Asociación Psicoanalítica de Buenos Aires*, 23 (3): 615–624.

Lacan, J. (1986). *The Ethics of Psychoanalysis, 1959–1960:. The Seminar of Jacques Lacan*. Translated by Dennis Porter. London and New York: W.W. Norton, 1992 [*Seminario 7. La ética del psicoanálisis*. Buenos Aires: Paidós, 1988].

Lacan, J. (1988). The family complexes in the formation of the individual. Translated by C. Asp. *Critical Texts*, 5 (3): 12–29 [*La familia*. Barcelona and Buenos Aires: Argonauta, 2003].

Laplanche, J. (1987). *New Foundations for Psychoanalysis*. Translated by David Macey. New York: Basil Blackwell, 1989 [*Nuevos fundamentos para el psicoanálisis. La seducción originaria*. Buenos Aires: Amorrortu, 1989].

Laplanche, J. (1996). El psicoanalista y su cubeta [Psychoanalysts and their cuvettes]. In: *Trabajo del Psicoanálisis*. Vol. I. Buenos Aires: Paidós, pp. 125–144.

Levin, R. (2002). Psicoanálisis: praxis de una ética: Diálogo con Raúl Levin [Psychoanalysis: Praxis of an Ethics. A Dialogue with Raúl Levin]. In: *Psicoanalistas: un retrato imposible* [Psychoanalysts: An Impossible Portrait]. Edited by S. Mauer, S. Moscona, and S. Resnizky. Buenos Aires: Lugar, pp. 151–152.

Levin, R. (2003). *Una perspectiva histórica y psicoanalítica sobre la "forma perspectiva"* [A Historical and Psychoanalytic Perspective on the "perspective form"]. Presented at the meeting of the Buenos Aires Psychoanalytic Association, Buenos Aires, April.

Levinas, E. (1969). *Totality and Infinity. An Essay on Exteriority*. Translated by Alphonso Lingis. Pittsburgh: Duquesne University Press.

Levinas, E. (1985). *Ethics and Infinity: Conversations with Phillipe Nemo*. Translated by Richard Cohen. The Hague and Pittsburgh: Martinus Nihjoff Publishers and Duquesne University Press [*Ética e infinito*. Madrid: La Balsa de la Medusa, 2000].

Levinas, E. (1986). The trace of the other. In: *Deconstruction in Context*. Edited by M. Taylor, Translated by Alphonso Lingis. Chicago: University of Chicago Press.

Lewkowicz, I. (2002). Reflexiones sobre la trama discursiva de la fraternidad [Some thoughts on the discursive weft of fraternity]. In: Droeven, J., ed., *Sangre o elección, construcción fraterna*, op. cit., pp. 247–296.

Bibliography

Liberman, A. (2002). Epílogo [Epilogue]. In: *Dispositivos clínicos en psicoanálisis*. Edited by S., Mauer, S. Moscona, and S. Resnizky. Buenos Aires: Letra Viva, pp. 203–207.

Luria, A. R. (1968). *A Little Book About a Vast Memory: The Mind of a Mnemonist*. Cambridge, MA: Harvard University Press.

Magris, C. (1999). *Utopía y desencanto* [Utopia and Disenchantment]. Translated by J. A. González Sainz. Barcelona: Anagrama, 2001.

Makintach, A. and Moscona, S. (2008). Sortilegios del amor [Love spells]. *Psicoanálisis de las Configuraciones Vinculares*, 31 (1): 83–105.

Mannoni, M. (1989). *De la pasión del ser a la locura del saber* [From the Passion of Being to the Madness of Knowing]. Buenos Aires. Paidós.

Marty, P. (2010). Essential depression. In: *Reading French Psychoanalysis*. Edited by D. Birksted-Breen, S. Flanders, and A. Gibeault. Translated by S. Leighton. Hove: Routledge. [La depresión esencial. In: *El orden psicosomático*. Valencia: Promolibro].

Masson, J. M. (Ed.) (1985). *The Complete Letters of Sigmund Freud to Wilhelm Fliess, 1887–1904*. Cambridge, MA: Harvard University Press.

Matus, S. (2003). Vínculo fraterno: de la legalidad paterna a la multiplicidad de legalidades [The fraternal link: From paternal law to multiple laws]. In: E. Berflein, et al., eds., *Entre hermanos: Sentidos y efectos del vínculo fraterno*, op. cit., pp. 9–46.

Matus, S. and Moscona, S. (1995). *Acerca de la desmentida y la vincularidad* [On Disavowal and Linking]. Presented at the AAPPG Conference, September.

Mauer, S. and May, N. (2012). *Clínica psicoanalítica de la parentalidad* [Psychoanalytic Practice and Parenting]. Presented at the Tercer Simposio Latinoamericano de Comunidad y Cultura [Third Latin American Symposium on Community and Culture], Buenos Aires, June and July.

Mauer, S., Moscona, S. and Resnizky, S. (2002). *Psicoanalistas: Un autorretrato imposible* [Psychoanalysts: An Impossible Self-Portrait]. Buenos Aires: Lugar.

Mauer, S., Moscona, S. and Resnizky, S. (2014). *Dispositivos clínicos en psicoanálisis* [Clinical Devices in Psychoanalysis]. Buenos Aires: Letra Viva.

May, N. and Mauer, S. (2003). La escritura psíquica en la infancia [Psychic writing in childhood]. *Revista de la Asociación Psicoanalítica de Madrid*, 39: 91–99.

McDougall, J. (1995). *The Many Faces of Eros: A Psychoanalytic Exploration of Human Sexuality*. New York: W.W. Norton. [*Las mil y una caras de Eros*. Buenos Aires: Paidós, 1998].

Meltzer, D. (1967). *The Psychoanalytic Process*. London: Heinemann.

Miller, J. A. (1991). *Lógicas de la vida amorosa* [The Logics of Love Life]. Buenos Aires: Manantial.

Miller, J. A. (1994). *Sujeto, goce, modernidad. Fundamentos de la clínica II* [Subject, Jouissance, Modernity: Fundamentals of Clinical Practice II]. Buenos Aires: Atuel.

Moreno, J. (2010). *Tiempo y trauma, continuidades rotas* [Time and Trauma: Broken Continuities]. Buenos Aires: Lugar.

Moreno, J. (2014). *How We Became Human: A Challenge to Psychoanalysis*. Translated by Judith Filc. Lanham, MD: Rowman & Littlefield [*Ser Humano. La inconsistencia, los vínculos, la crianza*. Buenos Aires: del Zorzal].

Morin, E. (1992). From the concept of system to the paradigm of complexity. *Journal of Social and Evolutionary Systems*, 15 (4): 371–385.

Morin, E. (2008). *On Complexity*. Translated by Robin Postel and Sean Kelly. Cresskill, NY: Hampton Press, 2008 [Epistemología de la complejidad. En *Nuevos Paradigmas. Cultura y Subjetividad*. Buenos Aires: Paidós, 1995].

Moscona, S. (2003). *Vínculos de paridad* [Peer links]. In: E. Berflein, et al., eds., *Entre Hermanos*, op. cit., pp. 189–227,

Moscona, S. (2013). *Sufrimiento vincular* [Link Suffering]. Presented at APdeBA's Annual Symposium, Buenos Aires, October.

Nasio, J. (1996). *El libro del dolor y del amor* [The Book of Pain and Love]. Buenos Aires: GEDISA.

Nasio, J. (2007). *El dolor de amar* [The Pain of Loving]. Buenos Aires: GEDISA.

Nietzsche, F. (1874). *Untimely Meditations.* Translated by R. J. Hollingdale. Cambridge: Cambridge University Press.

Novoa Blanco, R. (2002). *Mi hermano* [My brother]. Available at https://narrativa breve.com/2014/09/microrrelato-de-rafael-novoa-mi-hermano.html.

Nunberg, H. and Federn, E., eds. (1962). *Minutes of the Vienna Psychoanalytic Society.* Vol. I. New York: International Universities Press.

Paz, R. (2008). *Cuestiones disputadas en la teoría y en la clínica psicoanalítica* [Disputed Issues in Psychoanalytic Theory and Practice]. Buenos Aires: Biebel.

Persia, M. (2012). *El psicoanálisis consuela con la idea que tenemos una vida interesante* [Psychoanalysis comforts us with the idea that we lead an interesting life]. Interview with Claudio Martyniuk. *Clarín* daily, 6/10. Available at www.clarin.com/zona/psicoanalisis-consuela-idea-vida-interesante_0_HJ_WjQQ2vmg.html

Pichon-Rivière, E. (1971). *Del psicoanálisis a la psicología social* [From Psychoanalysis to Social Psychology]. Buenos Aires: Galerna.

Pommier, G. (1996). *Nacimiento y renacimiento de la escritura* [Birth and Rebirth of Writing]. Buenos Aires: Nueva Visión.

Pontalis, J.-B. (2000). *Windows.* Translated by Anne Quinney. Lincoln, NE and London: University of Nebraska Press, 2003 [*Ventanas.* Buenos Aires: Topia, 2005].

Pontalis, J.-B. (2007). *Al margen de los días* [In the Margins of the Days]. Buenos Aires: Topia.

Pontalis, J.-B. (2012). *Avant* [Before]. Paris: Gallimard.

Puget, J. (2004). *Sentimiento de responsabilidad: un hacer común* [The Sense of Responsibility: A Shared Doing]. Annual lecture, Argentine Group Psychology and Psychotherapy Association, Buenos Aires.

Puget, J. (2013). *Realidad, experiencia, material psicoanalítico* [Reality, Experience, Clinical Material]. In the proceedings of the annual symposium: *Las realidades del psicoanálisis: teoría, clínica y transmisión* [The Realities of Psychoanalysis: Theory, Clinical Practice, and Transmission]. Buenos Aires: Asociación Psicoanalítica de Buenos Aires, pp. 274–282.

Puget, J. (2014). *Jugando con lo íntimo, lo privado, lo público* [Playing with the Intimate, the Private, the Public]. Presented at Psicoanálisis y el psicoanalizar en un mundo de cambio [Psychoanalysis and Psychoanalyzing in a Changing World]. APdeBA, Buenos Aires, April.

Puget, J. (2015). *Subjetivación discontinua y psicoanálisis. Incertidumbres y certezas* [Discontinuous Subjectivation and Psychoanalysis: Uncertainties and Certainties]. Buenos Aires: Lugar.

Rabinovich, D. (1990). *El concepto de objeto en la teoría psicoanalítica* [The Concept of Object in Psychoanalytic Theory]. Buenos Aires: Manantial.

Raitzin de Vidal, I. (2010). Clínica de lo traumático: la función del analista [Clinical aspects of trauma: the analyst's function]. *Psicoanálisis*, 32: 377–403.

134 Bibliography

Resnizky, S. (1988). *Supervisión o super-visión* [Supervision or Super-Vision]. Presented at the Latin American Candidates Congress, Sao Paulo, September.

Ricoeur, P. (2004). *Memory, History, Forgetting*. Translated by Kathleen Blamey and David Pellauer. Chicago and London: University of Chicago Press.

Ritvo, J. B. (2012). *Figuras de la feminidad* [Figures of Femininity]. Buenos Aires: Letra Viva.

Rodrigué, E. (1966). *El contexto psicoanalítico* [The Psychoanalytic Context]. Buenos Aires: Paidós.

Rosset, C. (2012). *The Real and Its Double*. Translated by Chris Turner. Chicago: The University of Chicago Press, 2012 [*Lo Real y su doble – ensayo sobre la ilusión*. Barcelona: Tusquets, 1996].

Rotenberg, E. and Agrest Wainer, B. (2010). *Homoparentalidades: Nuevas familias*, op. cit.

Sahovaler de Litvinoff, D. (2009). *El sujeto escondido en la realidad virtual: de la represión del deseo a la pornografía del goce* [The Subject Hidden in Virtual Reality: From the Repression of Desire to the Pornography of Jouissance]. Buenos Aires: Letra Viva.

Sandler, J. (1983). Reflections on some relations between psychoanalytic concepts and psychoanalytic practice. *The International Journal of Psychoanalysis*, 64: 35–45.

Saramago, J. (2005). *The Double*. Translated by Margaret Jull Costa. New York: Mariner Books.

Sibilia, P. (2008). *La intimidad como espectáculo* [Privacy as Spectacle]. Buenos Aires: Fondo de Cultura Económica.

Soler, C. (1988). *Estudios sobre las psicosis* [Studies on Psychoses]. Translated by Irene Agoff. Buenos Aires: Manantial.

Soler, C. (2000). *La maldición sobre el sexo* [The Curse upon Sex]. Translated by Horacio Pons. Buenos Aires: Manantial.

Spivacow, M. (2005). *Clínica psicoanalítica con parejas* [Psychoanalytic Clinical Practice with Couples]. Buenos Aires: Lugar.

Tarrab, M. (2009). *El psicoanálisis y la eficacia de la toxicomanía* [Psychoanalysis and the Efficacy of Substance Dependence]. Available at www.nel-mexico.org/articulos/seccion/textosonline/subseccion/Toxicomanias-y-Alcoholismo/24/El-psicoanalisis-y-la-eficacia-de-la-toxicomania.

Ungar, V. (2011). *Disruption and Working-Through in the Supervisory Process*. Presented at the 47th IPA Congress, Mexico City, August.

Vainstoc, R. M. (2003). El porvenir del "acto clínico de fin de análisis" [The future of the "clinical act of the end of analysis"]. *Revista de psicoanálisis*, 40 (2): 427–453.

Valeros, J. (1997). *El jugar del analista* [The Analyst's Play]. Buenos Aires: Fondo de Cultura Económica.

Virno, P. (1999). *Déjà Vue and the End of History*. Translated by David Broder. London: Verso, 2015.

Weber, P. (2011). "Confused by all the new Facebook genders? Here's what they mean." Blogpost. In *Lexicon Valley: A Blog about Language* by Peter Weber. Available at www.slate.com/blogs/lexicon_valley/2014/02/21/gender_facebook_now_has_56_categories_to_choose_from_including_cisgender.html

Yerushalmi, Y. H. (1988). *Usos del olvido*. Buenos Aires: Ediciones Nueva Visión, 2006.

Yerushalmi, Y. H. (1991) *El Moisés de Freud. Judaísmo terminable e interminable*. Buenos Aires: Ediciones Nueva Visión, 1996.

Yourcenar, M. (1974). Reflections on the composition of *Memoirs of Hadrian*. In *Memoirs of Hadrian*. Translated by Grace Frick in collaboration with the author. New York: Farrar, Straus and Giroux, pp. 317–347 [Apostillas. In: *Memorias de Adriano*. Translated by Julio Cortázar. Buenos Aires: Sudamericana, 1981].

Zukerfeld, R. and Zonis Zukerfeld, R. (2013). *El problema del autor en la formación psicoanalítica: pluralismo riguroso e inconoclastia respetuosa* [The Problem of the Author in Psychoanalytic Training: Rigorous Pluralism and Respectful Iconoclasia]. Psychoanalytic Training Today Award, 48th IPA Congress, Prague, July.

Index

Note: Numbers in *italic* indicate a figure on the corresponding page.

absence-presence 34
adolescence 15, 29, 37, 73, 80, 111; and
    sexualities today 91–92
Agamben, G. 8, 80
alterity 33, 59–60, 63, 73
Assoun, P.-L. 44, 64
asymmetry 45, 65, 98
autobiography 123–125

Berenstein, Isidoro 33, 122
between, the 120
Bion, W. 1, 109
Bleger, J. 12, 19n2
Bleichmar, S. 97–98

capitalism 22
cartographies 10–11
clinical devices 1, 3, 10–19, 25, 75
clinical narratives 13–19, 26–27, 49–59;
    couples in conflict 32–35, 39–41;
    the fraternal dimension 66–71;
    sexualities 90–92, 96–98; the suffering
    of couples and families 22–24
complexity 1–2, 10, 12–13, 19–20;
    and the between 119; and
    clinical interventions 59; and
    couples in conflict 32, 34; and the
    fraternal dimension 74; and the
    psychoanalyst's writing process 104,
    106; and siblings 44
computers 81
connectivity 1, 34
control analysis 110–111
couples 2–4, 17–19, 29, 111–112; in
    conflict 31–41; and sexualities 97–98,
    99n6; the suffering of 20–25

Dalí, Salvador 47–48
deconstruction 1, 86, 88, 98–99
deficit 77–81
Deleuze, G. 2, 9–11
depression 15, 22, 73; essential
    depression 61n2
Derrida, J. 1, 10, 83, 126
devices 4, 43, 63, 84; and the between
    125; and clinical interventions 50–51,
    59–61; and family practice 27–30;
    institutional 121; philosophies of
    7–9; psychoanalytic 10–11, 13, 19, 21,
    25, 60, 108, 116; and sexualities 99; as
    a skein 9–10; *see also* clinical devices;
    sexuality device
disjunction, logic of 1, 51, 81
diversity 1–2, 4, 11, 13, 32, 48; and
    the between 120–121; and the
    fraternal dimension 73; and the
    psychoanalyst's writing process
    104, 106; and sexualities 90, 92; and
    supervision 110
domination 7, 46, 99
drawings 52, 54–57, *55–56*, 61n4,
    70–71, *70*

emotional dams 92
ethics 33, 46, 79, 81, 97; and the between
    119, 123; and the fraternal dimension
    73–74; and supervision 108
event 1, 3, 31, 34, 50, 64–65; *hermanarse*
    54, 57, 76n5, 119; and memory and
    forgetting 83, 86–87
excess 58, 60, 73, 77–81; excessive control
    28, 50; excessive stimuli 67; excess
    positivity 22; excess suffering 20

Index 137

face 68–71, *69*, 74, 76n3, 84
families 2–4, 8, 17–19, 22–24; and the between 119; and clinical interventions 50–54, 59–61; and couples in conflict 33, 38–41; and deficit and excess 80; family configurations 4, 92–98; and the fraternal dimension 66–68; and immobility 13–16; and memory and forgetting 84–85; and sexualities 89, 92–93; suffering of suffering 20–25; *see also* family practice; siblings
family practice 26–30, 44
fellow being 2, 21, 59, 97; and the between 118–121, 123; and the fraternal dimension 62–64, 70–71, 73, 76
Ferenczi, S. 76n2, 126
Fernández, A. M. 10, 98
Fiorini, Glocer 92
focal points of resistance 7
forgetting 84–87, 88n2
Foucault, M. 1, 45, 77; and clinical devices 7–11, 19; and sexualities 89–91, 98–99
frame *see* setting
fraternal collectives 119–121
fraternal complex 43, 71
fraternal dimension 62–64, 119–120; band of brothers 65–67; identical twin brothers 67–71; and the notion of trauma 64–65; and responsibility 73–76; in social ties 71–73
fraternal links *see* link
fraternal partnership 67, 72, 75–76
fraternity 42, 59, 65, 68, 114, 119; and parity 123; as responsibility 73–76
Freud, S. 2, 10–13, 21, 31, 42–44, 46–47; and the between 118–119, 122, 126; and deficit and excess 78; and the fraternal dimension 62–65, 69–71, 75; and memory and forgetting 82–83, 85–86; and the psychoanalyst's writing process 107; and supervision 108–109, 117n1

Gaspari, R. 45
Green, André 106–107
Green, Julen 122

Han, Byung-Chul 22
hands 54, *55*, 70, 105

helplessness 16, 73, 104, 115, 121; and clinical interventions 51, 60; and the fraternal dimension 63, 65–66
heterogeneous network 7
Hilflozichkeit see helplessness
horizontal bonds 46
hospitality 10, 25, 46, 126

immobility 10, 12–16, 29, 59
inter-vision 111, 115

Juarroz, Roberto 103–104

Kaës, René 33, 36–38, 51, 119
Kovadloff, Santiago 80, 103, 124

Lacan, J. 42, 52, 61n3, 63
Laplanche, J. 12, 63–65, 97–98
Levinas, Emmanuel 68, 70–71, 75, 122
link 1, 8, 23–25, 28–29; analytic link 10; and the between 118–122; and clinical interventions 58; and couples in conflict 31–32, 41; and deficit and excess 81; family link 119; fraternal-filial link 45, 54; fraternal link 42–46, 50, 54, 62–63, 65, 68, 71–74, 114, 123; hospitality link 126; link conflicts 20; link construction 21; link death 22; link device 17, 21, 60; link horizons 73; link interventions 40; link interviews 15; link logic 4, 21; link mode 7, 40; link organization 20; link pathology 20; link psychoanalysis 3–4, 19–21, 40, 48, 50–52, 60–61; link realities 34, 38; link responsibility 61; link suffering 20–22; link theory 2–3, 33–34, 59; link work 13, 16, 52, 60; and memory and forgetting 83–84; parental link 51; parent-child link 27, 45, 51, 59, 119; peer link 120; and the psychoanalyst's writing process 103; and sexualities 96–97; in the supervision space 108–117

McDougall, J. 97
memory 63, 65, 87–88, 107; as construction 82–85; *see also* forgetting
microphysics 7
Miller, J. A. 79
Moreno, J. 44, 87
Morin, E. 59

138 Index

mourning 9, 17, 21–22, 59–60, 104
multitasking 81

names 110–112, 115, 120
narcissism 44, 60, 78, 119, 123; and
  couples in conflict 31, 35, 38; and
  the fraternal dimension 70; and
  supervision 113–114, 116
narratives *see* clinical narratives
Nebenmensch see fellow being

object 9, 21, 31, 62–65, 97, 104
object relations 2
object series 52–59, *53, 55–56*
Oedipus complex 3, 38, 42, 44, 97
other, the 1–2, 10, 14, 20–24, 33; and
  the between 118–120, 122; and
  clinical interventions 49–51, 60;
  and the fraternal dimension 63, 75;
  and memory and forgetting 86; and
  sexualities 97; and siblings 45–46, 48;
  and supervision 108, 114

parity 42, 45, 59, 119–120, 123
Pichon-Rivière, E. 1–2, 77
Pontalis, J.-B. 30, 82–83, 86, 120, 122
positivity, excessive 22
presentation 1, 34
psychic pain 20, 41, 109
Puget, Janine 2, 21, 33, 74, 122

Rabinovich, Diana 63
representation 2, 9, 34, 40; and clinical
  interventions 51, 59, 61, 61n2; and
  the fraternal dimension 63–64, 73;
  and sexuality 98–99
responsibility 16, 18–19, 61, 79, 81; and
  the between 118–119, 125; fraternity
  as 73–76
re-view 111
Ricoeur, P. 86–87
Rodrigué, E. 60
Rosset, C. 71

self-management 18, 114–115, 119
sets 2, 8, 12, 39, 73–74; and clinical
  interventions 52, 54, *56*
setting 10, 12–13
sexualities 91–99; *see also* sexuality
  device
sexuality device 89–91

siblings 2–4, 42–48, 80, 123; and
  clinical devices 8, 13, 16, 18; and
  clinical interventions 51–54, 58–59;
  and couples in conflict 34–35, 38,
  40–41; and family practice 28–29; *see
  also* fraternal dimension
social ties 33, 71–73
Soler, C. 71, 97
solidarity 44–45, 59, 76–77, 117, 125
style 115, 120
subjectivity 1–3, 7, 10, 22, 25; and
  clinical interventions 50, 59; and
  couples in conflict 34; and deficit
  and excess 79; and the fraternal
  dimension 65, 71, 73, 75; and the
  psychoanalyst's writing process
  105; and sexualities 91, 95, 97; and
  siblings 43, 45, 48
suffering 4, 29, 52; and clinical devices
  10–11, 16; clinical perspectives on
  12–13; of couples and families 20–25;
  and couples in conflict 38, 40–41;
  and deficit and excess 80
supervision 4, 89, 108–117; self-
  supervision 105
symmetry 45, 71, 72; *see also*
  asymmetry

Tesone, J. E. 80
transmission 11, 15, 109–116
trauma 9, 31, 35, 43, 48, 61n2; and band
  of brothers 65–67; Ferenczi on 76n2;
  and the fraternal dimension 62; and
  the fraternal in social ties 73; and
  fraternity as responsibility 74–75;
  and identical twin brothers 67–71;
  on the notion of 64–65
twins 13, 42–43, 46–48, 66–71

Ungar, Virginia 109–110

violence 7, 22, 27, 43; and clinical
  interventions 49, 51–52, 58–61;
  and deficit and excess 79; and the
  fraternal dimension 65, 70–71, 74

web, the 8, 11–12, 51, 79, 92
writing 57–59, 83–84, 103–107,
  123–125

Yerushalmi, Y. H. 86